Gooseberry Patch

A Country Store In Your Mailbox℠

Old-Fashioned, Country Christmas

A holiday keepsake of recipes, traditions, homemade gifts, decorating ideas, & favorite childhood memories

Look for Vickie's & JoAnn's favorite recipes, merry-making ideas, and holiday survival hints sprinkled throughout this book.

A Country Store In Your Mailbox®

Gooseberry Patch
149 Johnson Drive
Department Book
Delaware, OH 43015

1·800·85·GOOSE
1·800·854·6673

Copyright 1995, Gooseberry Patch
0-9632978-0-5
Eighth Printing, August 1998

How To Subscribe

Would you like to receive
"A Country Store in Your Mailbox"℠?
For a 2-year subscription to our
Gooseberry Patch catalog
simply send $3.00 to:
Gooseberry Patch
149 Johnson Drive, Dept. Book
Delaware, OH 43015

CONTENTS

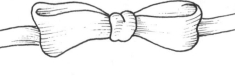

✌︎⁓ DEDICATION ⁓✌︎

This book is dedicated to everyone
who loves Christmas!

To our families, whose love and
encouragement to do the very best
we can is with us every day of our lives.

⁓ IN APPRECIATION ⁓

Our hearts go out to each and every
one of you who shared your family traditions,
recipes, and favorite holiday tips and ideas ~
you're what made this book possible. We were
overwhelmed by your response and generosity
in welcoming us into your lives and sharing
with us your warmest and most intimate
Christmas memories.

WELCOME HOME for The Holidays

For a very special effect, throw popcorn on your Christmas tree. Gives the look of freshly fallen snow!

Merideth Haus

String dried apple and orange slices for your country Christmas tree. Simply loop a piece of twine through the slice, hang and enjoy. It is also fun to dust the dried apples with cinnamon. They make the tree look and smell wonderful.

Make your own potpourri using dried apple slices, bay leaves, cinnamon sticks and nutmegs, and display in the glass globe of an old lantern. Finish off with a bow and greenery around the bottom for a great centerpiece. You can also make garlands for use all year long using the same materials. When decorating your kitchen for the holidays, hang the garlands in your kitchen windowsill or across the outside back of ladderback chairs.

Show off your prettiest potpourri in an old wooden butter mold.

ReDonna Newman

While visiting antique shops or flea markets, keep an eye open for chandelier prisms. After polishing, they make beautiful Christmas tree ornaments.

Snip herbs and tie in small bundles to dry. During the winter when the fireplace is in use, toss a bundle of herbs into the crackling fire for a wonderful scent. Try thyme, oregano, basil, sage or savory.

Joan Schaeffer

If sending large round cookies to a family member for Christmas, send them in an oatmeal or cornmeal container. They fit perfectly! Wrap the container with Christmas paper or have the kids draw, paint and decorate plain brown paper and wrap in that.

Lisa Murch

Use some favorites of your children's school projects to decorate your Christmas tree. From their first "masterpiece" to their kindergarten name tag, just use a hole punch and some Christmas ribbon.

Donna Page

Do some of your Christmas shopping through the mail. Looking through certain mail order catalogs can rival shopping at your favorite stores. Relax at home with a cup of tea, make your decisions over a period of a couple days or weeks, and choose from a wider selection than twenty stores have to offer, and have your packages delivered to your door. Yes, there are shipping charges to pay, but with what is gained in free time alone, it's worth it. And it's FUN!

Use a packaged gingerbread mix to make your gingerbread men. It makes delicious cookies with half the time and effort spent. Young children can help make the cookies and not be frustrated with measuring and waiting around for the real fun—decorating!

Joanne Martin-Robinson

Instead of tea or coffee at breaktime, bring along some hot cider mix; it's a great change.

Maria Vaz Duarte

Collect old tin graters and put votive candles inside for a wonderful Christmas glow (or anytime)!

Candace Daly

Celebrate Christmas in July! Rather than having your annual party in December when you're too overwhelmed to enjoy it, host a cookout in July with a Christmas theme, everything red and green! Serve bright juicy red watermelon, pink champagne, hot dogs with delicious salsa relish and a fresh crunchy green salad with red onion, red peppers, sliced apples and red wine vinegarette dressing. White twinkling lights, Christmas napkins and a small artificial tree decorated with take-home ornaments make for a very festive atmosphere.

WELCOME HOME for The Holidays

To make holiday napkin rings, use red and green curling ribbon to tie your napkins and decorate with holly or pine.

Include a family snapshot with all your cards for a personal touch.

Debbie Eng

String popcorn and cranberries on dental floss to decorate the Christmas tree. Thread a large sewing needle with waxed floss; it's very strong and the wax helps the popcorn and berries slide on easily. After the holidays, put the berry/popcorn garland on small trees or bushes as a special treat for the birds.

Brenda Radzinski

At work, enlist all interested personnel in a Secret Santa Society. Those interested submit their name, interests and favorite colors. Everyone participating draws a name. Monday through Thursday each secret santa leaves small gifts for their "friend." Have a Christmas coffee hour on Friday and reveal the santa identities by delivering a nice gift in person.

Donna Reynolds

With all the cooking during this time, you are bound to be using plenty of onions. To rid your hands of the smell, simply hold a stainless steel knife in both hands and run them under cold water. No more onion smell!

Linda Meyers

Place apples or oranges in your antique muffin tins and arrange with fresh greens and holly for a wonderful centerpiece.

Fill an old mason canning jar about 1/4 full of sand, and place a red votive candle in the center. Leave lid off and enjoy the flicker of candle-light!

Hang artificial garland (artificial greens) around the inside of your kitchen windows and place gingerbread cookies in amongst the greens. Looks adorable and your kitchen smells yummy.

Renee Murray

During the year, purchase holiday cookie cutters (especially when on sale). Using red, green, or plaid ribbon as a "hanger," display them on your tree. As holiday guests leave, each gets a cookie cutter along with a copy of your favorite cookie recipe, as a little token of a special time spent together.

Hang holiday cookie cutters with ribbon at your windows for a special touch. Tuck in a scoop of holiday potpourri tied in a piece of netting or lace to enjoy the "smells of the season."

Deborah Peters

Save your Christmas cards, especially those with notes about friends' activities, etc. Refer to them the following year when writing notes to far-away folks and friends. This lets your friends know you're interested in them!

Wrap gifts as you purchase them. Then there's no mad rush wrapping so many at once.

Joan Armstrong

Beginning in early December, mix up batches of cookie dough to pop in the freezer. Jot down rolling thickness, baking directions, etc. , on slips of paper and include them in the freezer bag. Saves hunting for the right cookbook! When cookies are needed, all you do is bake them. Lots of work and clean up time is saved!

Put the Christmas tree lights on a timer switch. That way you're not crawling over gifts Christmas Eve or morning to get the lights plugged in.

Sally Burke

Decorate cupcakes with green-tinted coconut arranged in wreath shape. Add cinnamon candies to look like holly berries.

Line gift cookie tins with clear fluorescent cellophane to add a sparkle to your goodies.

Karen Coll

Hang a sprig of holly from your bedpost and happy dreams will be yours!

WELCOME HOME for The Holidays

If your little ones find it hard to wait for Christmas morning gift opening, have Santa leave their stockings next to their bed during the night. Put little jingle bells on the stocking, so your child will hear Santa leave it.

Margaret Sullivan

Take your Christmas cards as they arrive and build a Christmas tree on the inside of your front door. Each time you go to answer the door, you will see all the warm wishes from family and friends. The very first card is the top of the tree.

Mildred Strobel

It's easy to forget, in times of relative peace, that there are thousands of servicemen and women away from home for the holidays, scattered to the ends of the earth. Start a new tradition and adopt a serviceperson **every** Christmas!

Forego office gifts completely and adopt a needy family. Prepare food baskets with contributions from your pantries at home. Pool the money that would have been spent on gifts for one another, to buy toys for the less fortunate.

Dawn Marshall

An excellent source for Christmas gift tags and for small gift wrapping paper is the folksy, whimsically Christmasy and countrified illustrated GOOSEBERRY PATCH mail order catalog. There are endless possibilities to create one of a kind gift wrap and gift tags. Another idea is to cut out Christmasy scenes, and red and green colored ads from the newspaper.

Jacqueline Wingard

Get out all your favorite yelloware, spatterware, saltglaze and woodenware bowls and fill to the brim with bright shiny red and green apples, walnuts and popcorn!

Make a tree skirt to remember your children or grandchildren. Choose a plain fabric, put a fringe or border on to your liking. With chalk, trace each child's handprint. Have the mother or you embroider the hand, child's name and year. You can add to this forever!

Pauline Williams

Give young friends and newly-weds "things of Christmas" as part of a wedding gift, birthday gift, etc. Give special ornaments, candles, santas and music boxes, so they can begin their own collections and traditions.

Leave two or three special Christmas things out year-round, to remind you that the spirit of Christmas should last all year.

Susan Andrews

Wrap your presents in brown paper, then have the kids pull out their crayons and write messages and draw holiday pictures. Then tie the packages with "ribbons" made from strips of calico.

Sandy Jean Tucker

When rolling out sugar cookies to cut, roll out on powdered sugar instead of flour. It works just as well and adds to the flavor just a bit more.

Bonnie Morris

If you receive many mail order catalogs, pick a favorite charity and have a gift sent there. For example, send a box of rawhide dog bones to the Humane Society for all the homeless animals at Christmas.

Maryann Szalka

Glue a miniature calendar to the inside cover of your checkbook. It saves time and prevents errors when dating checks.

Martha Davis

Prepare custom-tailored baskets for your friends to match their different personalities, life-styles and interests. These little theme-type baskets are a lovely gift idea.

Kristi Benefield

WELCOME HOME for The Holidays

Take beeswax santas and tie them to the chandelier, then twine variegated English ivy in and out around the santas. The bulbs should be above.

Carolyn Belzner

Christmas is a special time of year, so the most important thing to remember is to share the peace of the Lord, the "reason for the season." One good way to share is to give a small gift to someone who would least expect it from you.

It's always a good idea to keep an index card with shoe, shirt and pant sizes for spouses, parents, etc. When you go out shopping you'll then have the vital information.

Laura Forman

A must for holiday entertaining or mood music is **George Winston - December** on Windham Hill Productions. This is a collection of piano solos.

Rebecca Ilgen

A great way to avoid those crazy, stressful shopping malls during the holidays is to give homemade coupons. Fun to give as well as receive, coupons for cleaning someone's house, cooking a meal, watering their plants, giving a perm, grocery shopping, baking or walking the dog are always welcomed. Kids love making their very own coupons too. It's a fun, inexpensive and very personal gift to give. And don't forget gift certificates for favorite restaurants, haircuts and groceries as well as magazine and newspaper subscriptions!

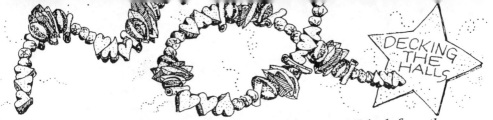

Take 5 quart ice cream pails and fill them with water 1/2 inch from the top. Set outside during freezing weather until the water freezes. It will take 5 hours or more in below freezing temperatures. The sides and top will freeze first. Just before the entire bottom freezes, turn the ice out of the bucket into the snow. Nestle the "ice candle" in gentle snow banks or along a walk or driveway. Then place a votive candle in the natural hollow in the center of the ice. Really an eye catcher!

Cindy Footit

Take a round twig basket and fill with a big tangle of shiny gold star garlands. Then stick a few little bits of greenery here and there along the edges. With candlelight reflecting off the shiny stars, it makes for a very enchanted room!

Place a Christmas tree (real or artificial) in each room of the house. Decorate each tree according to the theme of the room.

Take a large saucepan and fill it half full of water. Add whole cloves, cinnamon sticks, orange rind and allspice, and gently simmer. The whole house fills with a wonderful aroma, and the potion can be used again and again.

String tiny colored lights on an outside tree, bringing the Christmas spirit out to the backyard as well as inside. Turn the lights on in the afternoon and have fun watching the birds sit in the tree amongst the twinkling lights.

Debbie Clement

Make poinsettia cookies using any sugar cookie recipe, baked with a green stick (very smallest dowel rod). "Pot" in a decorative flower container with styrofoam painted with black frosting to represent dirt. What wonderful decorations and hostess gifts these make!

Carolyn Nelson

For the kids, bake a hard peppermint candy inside one chocolate cupcake. The lucky child that gets the cupcake wins a small gift. It's like a twelfth night cake with its penny, only totally edible.

Marlaine Pietrzak

WELCOME HOME for The Holidays

After hours of Christmas cookie baking, it's a nice touch for a child to be able to go to the freezer and pull out a moistened folded face cloth, which has been soaked in fresh lemon water. It's most refreshing to their little flour faces and hands.

Children can create fantasy sculptures from colored wooden toothpicks and colorful gumdrops and when they take them apart, they can eat them!

Heat paraffin (and old candles with crayons added for color) in a heavy pan. Pour an inch into metal muffin tins. Set a medium-size pinecone into each cup, bottom first, and stand straight. When cooled completely, remove and you have firestarters for your fireplace that are quite pretty and practical.

During the year, purchase pretty, unusual and inexpensive china or glass plates at flea markets, garage and estate sales. Use them for your many cookie exchanges during the holidays. They are lovely when tied with fabric bows and much more special than paper plates.

Jan Kouzes

Take colored glass mason jars and place three different sizes in one corner of your kitchen counter. Put a string of white lights in them, add a few sprigs of holly and some red ribbon. The result is beautiful.

Bonnie Froehlich

No one is busier during the holidays than the lady of the house. A nice thing to do is have a Christmas Coffee, some morning around the first week in December. It's a nice break for the guests while out shopping, to stop for coffee and pastry and chat for awhile, and it puts everyone in the holiday mood.

Shirley Carmack

14

Display Christmas packages in an antique trunk or basket. It keeps gifts tidy and creates a country Christmas feeling.

Take a favorite country stoneware bowl and fill it with greens topped with pomegranates and/or red apples.

Create ribbons and bows from your favorite country fabric by cutting it into strips. It's less expensive than yards of ribbon. One square yard of fabric will decorate the whole house. Fringed edges of fabric ribbons retain a country flavored homespun look.

Get out the children's stuffed animals, well loved and not so loved, and dress them in mufflers and stocking caps. Stack them in a corner, in an antique trunk or under the tree.

Children love to help decorate at Christmas. Place a small live or artificial tree in their rooms and let them trim the tree with a favorite collection.

Make the wassail bowl more festive by encompassing it with a grapevine wreath, decorated with red ribbon flowing through its branches.

Take bundles of 4 to 6 inch cinnamon sticks and tie with homespun ribbon. Fill a basket or set individually on an end table or atop a bookcase or desk.

Decorate a tree with naturals such as red cockscomb, golden yarrow, hydrangea, baby's breath and pinecones.

Stephanie Kurth

Simmer some cinnamon oil diluted with water. It gives a wonderful Christmas smell!

Cindy Ricke

Learn to say "no." We all try to do more than is humanly possible during the holidays. Don't feel as though you have to do everything. Pick a few things you really want to do and indulge yourself with those things. If you love decorating, go all out. But simplify some other things like buying your holiday cookies at a bakery, computerizing your Christmas letter or meeting your friends at a favorite restaurant rather than hosting your own holiday party.

WELCOME HOME for The Holidays

Invite 10 friends over for a candy and ornament exchange. Each guest brings 10 pieces of homemade Christmas candy and 10 handmade ornaments. After the exchange, share candy recipes and directions for making the ornaments. A fun time especially when held in early December, so the guests have time to experiment on their own before the holidays. Each guest goes home with 10 pieces of candy and 10 new ornaments.

Have a potpourri get-together. Have each guest bring pinecones, cinnamon sticks, lemon peels, orange peels, cloves, nutmeg, peppermint leaves, etc. Mix all together with some potpourri oil of your choice. Fill small bags so each guest can take home a sample. Tie each bag with bright ribbon and a tag listing all the ingredients.

Mabel Lamb

A nice way to spend Christmas Eve is to have each family member share a favorite memory of times past, read a short story or poem, or sing a Christmas song.

I AM CHRISTMAS

I am mistletoe and kisses and warm winter wishes.

Jack Frost in the air and snow in your hair.

Children gazing at toys, happy girls and boys.

Santas in department stores and holly wreaths decorating doors.

Bells ringing and carolers singing.

Festive foods and many friends in happy moods.

I am a part of these many, many things.

Why?

Because, I am Christmas!

Susan Smithee

Decorate a window ledge with pine, ribbon and gingerbread men.

Before using pinecones for a wreath or other Christmas decorations, place them in a warm oven for about an hour. The heat makes them open up.

Jodie Shultz

On cold mornings around the holidays, put green food coloring in oatmeal for your children and grandchildren. Cinnamon sprinkled on top adds a festive touch.

Jackie Stephens

String pretty Christmas ribbon or yarn across windows, and hang Christmas cards on it to create a "garland."

Bake homemade yeast sweet rolls and deliver to friends and neighbors on Christmas Eve day, in time to eat on Christmas morning.

Have a "beverage exchange" instead of a cookie exchange. Homemade eggnog, cider with cinnamon sticks, herb teas and gourmet coffee beans in mason jars or pitchers are lovely gifts.

If you have elderly neighbors (and willing teenagers in the family), give coupon books for snow shoveling, taking out the garbage, etc. They can be redeemed in the winter months when it is icy and slippery outside.

Invite friends and family to church for Christmas Eve services. If it weren't for Jesus' birth, we'd have nothing to celebrate.

Let the children arrange the nativity figures in the creche scenes.

Make or buy a fabric colored photo album (Christmas colors of course!) and keep your Christmas photos separate from the rest, by putting them in this album. Set it out on the coffee table at Christmas and let everyone see how the family has changed and grown.

Beth Prinz

Special touches for the holidays for guest rooms include fresh flowers, electric tea kettle, china cups, a basket of special teas and instant coffees, fresh fruit, magazines and extra quilts and cozy blankets.

WELCOME HOME for The Holidays

Poinsettias are poisonous to our animal friends and can cause great harm it eaten. Purchase silk poinsettias instead, as they will last forever and will not make our animals sick.

If you are considering getting a pet, go to your local animal shelter. When you adopt one of these animals, you will be saving its life.

If you happen to see a starving and neglected animal this holiday season, open your heart and your home to help him. He will be eternally grateful for your kindness and you will be doing a wonderful thing.

Michelle Gardner

Place sprigs of Christmas tree into old potpourri for a fresh holiday fragrance.

Chris Serbia

Think "real" versus "toy" items for some childrens' presents, like real cookie cutters, rolling pins and measuring cups instead of toy versions. Receiving these is much more thrilling to a child and they last longer too.

Take a family walk around the neighborhood just before bed on Christmas Eve. The anticipation and magic in the air is electric.

Vicki Wilkes

Animals have Christmas traditions all their own. So the legend goes, for one hour on Christmas Eve, all animals can speak.

18

DECKING THE HALLS

When making cakes or cookies for Christmas presents, wrap the boxes in butcher or plain paper, and decorate with the recipe of the contents. This way the person knows what food is inside and the proper care it should be given.

Raylene Nunes

To freshen up mashed bows, use a curling iron.

Cheryl Parker

Gather together a group of friends and a pick-up and go carolling. Visit the homes of friends unable to participate, senior citizen homes or housing projects. With a bale or two of straw in the bed of the pick-up, you'll think you're on a hayride!

Donna Fox

Tuck small sprays of fresh baby's breath in Christmas greenery, wreaths and garlands for extra sparkle. If carefully put away, the dried baby's breath can be used again and again.

Terri Harvey

Collect apothecary jars and fill with all kinds of goodies. Red and green candies, candy-coated milk chocolates, foil-wrapped candies, gumdrops, hard candies, etc., and tie with a Christmas ribbon around the neck. The larger jars can be used for cookies. When the jars are lined up on the hutch, they make a very attractive arrangement.

Eleanor Oliver

A busy mom/housewife likes nothing better than the gift of time. Make a certificate good for free babysitting and give mom a break.

Giving a bridal shower before the holidays? Ask each guest to attach an ornament to their gift. The new couple will have enough decorations for their first tree together.

Save old Christmas cards for nursing/rest homes. They often use them for arts and crafts projects.

Teresa Labat

WELCOME HOME for The Holidays

Have your children make sugar cookie cut-outs and decorate them. Then hang them in the window panes.

Trim your window sills with fresh greens and berries, warmed by votive candles. Enjoy the scent!

Tessa Adelman

In the kitchen, suspend an evergreen garland from and around the lighting in the ceiling. Then hang small wooden and metal kitchen ornaments, gingerbread men, candy canes and cookie cutters from the garland. It makes the kitchen very festive.

Jeanne Bliss

Mix potpourri, hard candies, or sprigs of fragrant greenery with packing materials when preparing a gift for shipping. It adds a festive and aromatic touch for the recipient.

Each day you open a "door" on your Advent calendar, you or all family members drop coins into a Christmas stocking or other Christmas container. Near the holiday, the family can together make a monetary contribution to its favorite charity.

Michele Melander

Line the front and back stairs with poinsettias and alternate with a teddy bear. You could also put the poinsettias in a bag and tie with raffia and cinnamon hearts.

Elizabeth Fox

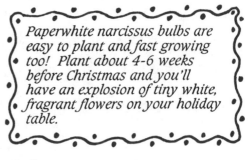

Paperwhite narcissus bulbs are easy to plant and fast growing too! Plant about 4-6 weeks before Christmas and you'll have an explosion of tiny white, fragrant flowers on your holiday table.

Think of the people you usually complain to, then turn the tables a bit. Call up your doctor just to say, "I wonder how you're feeling and happy holidays." Leave a plate of cookies out for the mail carrier and give the trash collector a gift.

Lynda Zimmer

For a country/Victorian look, instead of using tinsel on your Christmas tree, decorate the tree with baby's breath. One bunch is enough for an average size tree.

Denise Harrison

Bake several batches of any favorite bread: pumpkin, apple, banana nut or any quick bread mix. Bake according to recipe but instead of a pan, bake the loaves in any size glass canning jar! Grease the jar and fill a little less than half full. Put the filled jars on a cookie sheet and bake. After cooled, put on the rings and lids and add some decoration. The bread looks and tastes extra special and will keep several days.

Keep a large bowl full of popcorn and one of fresh cranberries under your tree. All your visitors, and the children, will love to string these and place on outdoor evergreens for the birds and squirrels. And it keeps kids busy for hours!

Sharon Holmes

For those relatives far away at holiday time, make a video tape of your family in front of the Christmas tree, opening the gifts those relatives sent. Include personal messages and then send a copy of the tape to these special people.

Susan Thompson

If you run out of ideas on what to get someone who has everything, try a fruit basket. A fruit basket has something for young and old alike. And they're colorful and yummy too!

Sharon Hall
Gooseberry Patch

Cherish all your happy moments—they make a fine cushion for old age.

Ramona Mullins

WELCOME HOME for The Holidays

Meatloaf will not stick to the pan if you place a slice of bacon on the bottom of the pan before baking.

LaVerne Biunno

Invite several friends over for a "silent auction." Everyone brings a handmade gift. Gifts are displayed on a table with a piece of paper and pencil near each. For 5 minutes each guest walks around the table writing their "silent bid" on the paper for that item, with their initials. When the time is up, everyone anxiously rushes to see what they won. The money collected is sent to a favorite charity. It's a great way to share handcrafted gifts with friends, and share with those less fortunate too.

Lisa Prichard

Pets like Christmas too! When visiting friends during the holidays, remember to wrap up a few treats for their pet. Both pet and owner will be pleasantly surprised.

Patty Zielinski

Hang your metal cookie cutters from your window grids using red and green yarn. They add a homespun touch to your kitchen and family room.

Linda Holderle

When making handmade gifts for close friends, keep a file box with their names, the year, and what you made. This way you don't make the same gift the next year, and it eliminates having to try and remember from year to year.

Donna Weidner

Use red and green candy-coated milk chocolate candies instead of chocolate chips when making your favorite chocolate chip cookie recipe. Festive as well as yummy!

Patricia Loughren

Place pomanders in your apple stacker, sit them in a bed of bay leaves, or hang them from your Christmas tree. They look and smell great.

Patricia Lacefield

Purchase calendars for the new year and fill in birthdays, anniversaries and other important dates. Everyone really appreciates the gift and uses it all year long.

Kathy Jorgensen

Hang your crocheted snowflakes in a "drafty" spot, using clear fishing line. The wind movements create a snowfall effect. Beautiful!

When giving treats to older relatives, put them on a colorful plastic plate or tray. Glass ones are pretty, but sometimes a little too heavy for frail hands.

Cindy Wattenschaidt

When sending letters or cards, sprinkle a little cinnamon-scented pot-pourri in the envelope. A very nice touch!

Fill bags with special gifts for friends. Include stoneware ornaments, cookie cutters, beeswax candles and ornaments, country notepads, Christmas potholders, homemade potpourri, cinnamon ornaments, or anything country or primitive to suit the special person.

Place many small trees around the house. Use feather trees and small pine trees decorated with sweet annie and other natural things, small baskets, beeswax ornaments, candles, homespun skirts, old toys—the list is endless!

Joyce Newburn

A lovely dessert treat for your Christmas dinner is to make ice cream figures (santas, snowmen, snowballs) and place them on a bed of spun sugar.

Ann Jackson

Christmas is the time to bring out your favorite embroidered linens, bedding and table dressings.

WELCOME HOME for The Holidays

God's little creatures enjoy Christmas too! Make special holiday treats for birds and assorted wildlife—a mixture of cranberries, sunflower seeds, suet, raisins, peanuts, and of course, gooseberries.

Jan Gajowski

To make the animals for Noah's Ark tree, use cookie cutters to trace onto heavy brown grocery bags.

Laurie Keep

Remember the birds at Christmas. Decorate a tree with small suet balls and other goodies. Use a tree in the yard, or put one on a patio. It's fun to watch!

Billie Jane Berndt

To make your Christmas tree at work more special, ask each employee to bring in two **homemade** ornaments, instead of buying commercial ones. You'll end up with a very special tree.

Anne Cartwright

CHRISTMAS: When Paradise comes to Earth.

Debra Himes

Every year have a name exchange for your extended family. Each person makes a gift for the person whose name he/she drew. (Men participate too!) Opening each other's handmade gifts is the highlight of the exchange. Keep a list of what was made from year to year.

Pam Bartholomew

Use an extra room in your home to be "Santa's Workshop." The children will have to stay out so that the elves can work. It will provide you with a workspace that you don't have to tidy up each day.

Elizabeth Heyman

A good way to store those extra-small ornaments is to place them in individual sections of an egg carton.

Phyllis Frump

If you have toddlers in your home, make all of your Christmas tree decorations out of calico. Make stars, hearts and snowmen to put on the tree so if they fall off when a branch is tugged, nothing will break. As the kids grow, add more fragile ornaments to your living room tree, and pass the fabric ones on to the kids to use on a "children's tree." They'll really enjoy decorating a small tree all their own.

Put a small cedar tree in the kitchen and decorate it with cinnamon hearts and stars, homespun stuffed fabric hearts and popcorn strings. Place it in a pretty crock or drape homespun around the base.

Have one little area of your home that you change seasonally, perhaps in the entryway. You can go from hearts and valentines on February 14th, to flags on July 4th, to pumpkins and Indian corn in October, to your favorite Christmas mini quilt.

Roseann Wood

Address your Christmas cards in January or February each year and then fill them out closer to the holidays. It saves alot of time and work.

Pegi Jenkins

A great gift to give your parents is a weekend away. All the children chip in and send them to a resort for a mini-vacation. Add some extra money for a fancy meal out on the town. To tell them what their gift is you could write a poem describing it. Let their employers in on the scheme so that time off can be scheduled accordingly.

Sarah Austad

Take all your cookie-making stuff to grandma's and "let her help." In a pinch you could even take ready-made refrigerated dough. No one cares since the fun is in the decorating!

Eileen Clark

WELCOME HOME for The Holidays

At holiday time, take extra food from your pantry and donate it to local food banks. You can restock and your canned, nutritious food is then never thrown away.

Save one small, wrapped gift (action toy, sketching book and pens, cars) for each child, until about a week after Christmas. Then "find" it in your closet and tell them it must have gotten lost when the presents were brought out. It helps alleviate the "let down" that many of the kids experience after Christmas is over.

Do your major cookie baking or gingerbread house building AFTER Christmas. The major rush is over, the kids are on vacation and have nothing to do, so it will be enjoyed much more. The cookies can go in the freezer for lunch treats and there won't be so many sweets all at the same time.

An idea if you have a large collection of santas, would be to have an "Advent Santa." Put a new one out each day until the REAL Santa comes.

Donna Alongi

Take an old tin muffin pan and fill each cup with a votive candle. The warm glow from the shimmering light will brighten any room and fill it with a cozy, holiday feeling.

Sharon Leinbach

Keep an old candle stub in your recipe box and when you write out a new recipe, rub the candle briskly over the card. Spills wipe off easily and it keeps the card from smudging.

Anne Legan

Make your own homemade gift tags! Take last year's Christmas cards and with pinking shears cut pictures from fronts of cards. Then take plain white paper with pinking shears, cut backs for your front pictures a little larger than the fronts. Punch two holes in top of fronts with backs attached and tie with red or green ribbon.

Judy Schram

Fill an old sleigh, wagon or bench with holiday packages. It's a great way to "Christmas up" the outside of your house.

GiVING...

THE MEANING OF CHRISTMAS

Gifts To Make
IN A
TWINKLING

Giving... The Meaning of Christmas

Cow Wrapping Paper

ReDonna Newman

For all of you who love cows, use white shelf paper, draw on the black cow spots with a black marker and use as gift wrap. Tie the packages with red curly ribbon.

Christmas Potpourri

Joan Schaeffer

6 thin-skinned oranges
10 cinnamon sticks
cloves
2 oz. orange oil
6 drops cinnamon oil

Use a potato peeler to make long strips, about 1/2" wide, from the oranges. Stud the peels with cloves, 1/2"-1" apart. Pour orange oil and cinnamon oil in a bowl and dip peels in oil. Allow excess to drip off rind. Dip cinnamon sticks in mixture as well. Place potpourri in an attractive glass or ceramic bowl and enjoy! This recipe can easily be doubled or tripled so make a large batch to have on hand for gifts. Should the scent diminish, reapply oil mixture to peels.

Surround your holiday punch bowl with greenery, berries, shiny red apples, golden pears and spicy pomanders!

Christmas Pinecones

Joan Schaeffer

Soak pinecones in any of the following solutions. When the pinecones are thrown into your fireplace fire, they will burn different colors.

1/2 lb. soda to 1/2 gallon water or
1/2 lb. borax to 1/2 gallon water or
1/2 lb. salt to 1/2 gallon water

After soaking pinecones in any of above solutions overnight, remove from solution and place in mesh bags to dry thoroughly.

Grandparents' Gifts

Shirley Ainsworth

Have your children make and decorate their own Christmas cards shaped as santa, a Christmas tree, gingerbread house or such. Paste a picture inside of the child or the child with grandparent. Then have the child write a sentence and sign. It will become a treasured gift and could even be framed.

Homemade Stationery

Eileen Clark

Make stationery for teachers, grandmas and others using rubber stamps and bulk-bought note pads. You can buy 12 in a package very inexpensively. Put strip magnets on back, so this handy gift can go on the fridge.

Holiday Card & Goody Holders

Louise Wheeler

With recycling on everybody's mind, here is an idea for reusing empty detergent and cereal boxes. I made my first holiday card and goody holder over 25 years ago, when my son and daughter were little. The first one I made was for Valentine's Day and it was decorated with hearts, and hung on their doorknob and in the morning on Valentine's Day, they found their cards, candy and trinkets inside. I also did one for Halloween and decorated it with pumpkin faces. Use your imagination—it's fun to design one for every holiday!

GiViNG...THE MEANiNG of CHRiStMAS

Pinecone Bird Treat
Donna Alongi

Push bread crumbs or peanut butter and birdseed into a pinecone, then hang it outside. It is a fun way to give the birds a holiday treat.

Unique Wooden Ornaments
Cindy Wattenschaidt

If you enjoy woodworking, each year you could make a unique ornament symbolizing an important event of that year, like cradles and rocking chairs when children are born or school buses when they start school. Use your imagination to create treasures for your tree!

Inexpensive Gift Wrap
Lynda Zimmer

For inexpensive gift-wrapping, save mail order catalogs and cut out the beautiful color covers. Then paste on to white shelf paper.

Handmade Christmas Cards
Teresa Labat

Let your children take turns designing your own custom-made Christmas cards. Take their art work to the printers and you'll have a special greeting to send to friends and family.

Easy/Elegant Centerpiece
Lawrie Hamilton

For a quick and lasting centerpiece for the holiday dining table, place about 30 small pinecones in a large cardboard box. Using gold spray paint, cover the pinecones with color. Shaking the box occasionally helps to move the pinecones around to coat all exposed areas. Let pinecones dry thoroughly. Gather together a crystal bowl, some gold or colored Christmas bulbs, several yards of gold ribbon and those gold stars on wire (so common now for holiday decorating). Crystal candlesticks with holiday candles may be added. When pinecones are dry, arrange some of them, with bulbs, in the bowl and set bowl in the center of the table. Surrounding the bowl, arrange some more pinecones, the ribbon and two foot lengths of the gold star wires, twisted to form pleasing shapes. The addition of crystal candlesticks and candles amongst this arrangement gives added sparkle.

Paper Bows
Jan Ertola

For your Christmas tree, make red bows out of paper ribbon and tie them with wire. Each year, just wrap them around a tree branch. They can be used over and over again.

Mantle Decoration
Jeanne Traut

Take white shelf paper and cut a simple schereschnitte (or papercutting) along one edge. That edge hangs down and becomes a lacy border along the mantle. Then put pine boughs and other decorations on the mantle shelf.

Christmas Tablecloth
Ruth Huneke

Each year, have family members "sign" a plain tablecloth with indelible ink and date their drawings, signatures, whatever. Embroider these and you'll have a wonderful memory of all your Christmases together.

> *"Frost" oranges, lemons, limes, apples and grapes for holiday garnishes and centerpieces. Simply brush fresh fruit with beaten egg white then roll in sugar.*

Graham Cracker Gingerbread Houses

Sheryl Adams

These are so easy and fun for the children to do. They are made out of graham cracker squares "cemented" together with thick powdered sugar frosting (recipe on box). Make the roof by slanting two squares together. Decorate with various candies; candy-coated milk chocolates or gumdrops for the roof, hard rock candy for doors and windows, mini pretzels for a fence, upside down sugar ice cream cone for trees (iced with green frosting) and coconut for snow. Set all on a piece of cardboard covered with foil.

Here's our recipe for sturdy "Glue Icing" for gingerbread houses. Simply mix together 2 egg whites and 2 1/2 cups of confectioners sugar!

Tweet Hearts

Charlene Julian

You can give your feathered friends a treat this holiday season by following this simple recipe.

1 1/4 lb. suet
1/2 c. sunflower seeds

1/2 c. crushed peanuts
1/2 c. cracked corn kernels

Melt suet in oven or saucepan (yields about 2 c. liquid fat). Stir in peanuts, sunflower seeds and corn. Spoon mixture into 4-1 c. heart molds; insert a drinking straw at top (for hole). Cool in the refrigerator until solid. Unmold, remove straw, thread with string and tie to a shaded tree branch.

Recipe for "Christmas Fragrance". Simmer cinnamon sticks, lemon and orange peel, cloves and nutmeg. Instantly, your home will have the warm, cozy fragrance of the holidays!

Potato Stencil Gift Wrap
Valerie Bryan

Slice white potatoes in half. Make an imprint with a cookie cutter in the center of the potato. Cut away potato around design. Dip the raised design area in natural food coloring and press on white or brown paper. Makes a very pretty gift wrap for children's gifts.

Carol's Clay
Katherine Loope

1 1/2 c. water	1 T. vegetable oil
food coloring of your choice	1 t. alum
1/2 c. salt	1 1/2 c. flour

Bring water, vegetable oil and food coloring to a boil. Remove from stove. Add the alum, and then add the salt, stirring to dissolve as much as possible. Then add flour and knead until pliable. Use more flour if necessary. Store in a covered container. Keeps well for months. If you want, you can add 1 or 2 drops of scented oil.

Advent Calendar
Linda Wiley

Take a wooden dowel and attach a piece of felt over the top. Sew 25 pockets, numbered 1 through 25, onto the felt. Embroider your child's name at the top. Attach a length of yarn to each end of the dowel, so that your "calendar" can be hung. Each day in December place a candy, note or other surprise in the appropriate pocket as a countdown to the big day.

> *Do-it-yourself Christmas wrap! Cut simple designs (hearts, trees, stars) out of sponges. Dip designs into acrylic paint, blot once on newspaper and stamp out great designs on kraft or white shelf paper!*

Ragball Snowman

Connie Casteel

2 tiny black buttons (for eyes)
2 small branches (for arms)
1 small orange button (for nose)
12"(L) x 1"(W) strip of wool (for scarf)
several 18" strips of torn muslin
    (about 3/4" wide)

2" styrofoam ball
4" styrofoam ball
small straw broom

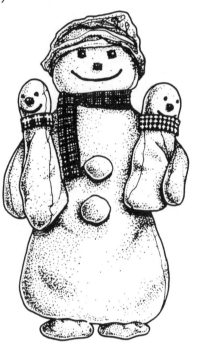

Wrap each styrofoam ball with strips of muslin until ball is completely covered. Place a toothpick in the middle of the larger ball and centering smaller ball over toothpick, push down until both balls are secured. Decorate face with buttons. (OPTIONAL: A small pipe can be made with clay and painted black, and placed in mouth area.) Wool strip used for scarf should be frayed on the edges to look like fringe. (OPTIONAL: Small black felt hat can be placed on his head.) Ragball snowman will add to your holiday decorations or can be kept out all year round—he won't melt!

Orange or Grapefruit Baskets

Jeanne Elmer

oranges or grapefruit
ice pick

jute
birdseed

Cut fruit in half and scoop out the pulp, or make juice in the juicer. Poke 2 holes in fruit on opposite sides with ice pick. Put jute through the holes and knot on the outside. Fill with birdseed and hang from your trees.

> *Recycle your Christmas tree! Some Park Departments will chip up your Christmas tree and you can take it home and use it for mulch.*

Country Christmas Arrangement *Teresa Shipp*

Fill the bottom of a shallow wooden box or basket with Spanish moss. Then arrange 3 to 5 oranges inside. Cut small, shallow holes in the tip of each orange. Place a short votive candle (the ones with metal on the bottom and sides) in each hole. Fill in around the oranges with fresh or artificial greenery. Add two or three small pinecones, then a simple raffia bow tied to the side. Light the candles right before the guests arrive.

Family Fan Mail *Karen Mauger*

Perfect if you have someone who is away from the family for the holidays, especially our servicepeople. You'll need a roll of brown paper, some marking pens and a mailing tube. Have everyone write a note, share family news, or let the little ones just scribble. Make a family tree on the front so the person knows just who everyone is. Then mail off your love on a roll, it's sure to be a hit.

Christmas Spirit Corsage *Patricia Kinghorn*

Take 2 to 3 pieces of boxwood (2 1/2" long) and tie with a red ribbon. Attach to coat with a hat pin. Instant Christmas spirit!

Christmas Basket *Patricia Kinghorn*

Use a straw basket or a small sleigh. Line basket with plastic wrap and fill with soaked oasis (can be found at florist shops or craft centers). To use oasis, cut dry block to fit container, remove block and soak it in water, then replace block. Fill container with evergreen clippings pushed into the oasis block (juniper, yew or boxwood). Add a sprig or two of holly, red berries and a Christmas bow. A lovely centerpiece that will stay fresh throughout the holiday season, just add water as necessary.

GiVING...THE MEANING of CHRISTMAS

Christmas Cookie Window Ornaments
Sandi Cargill

Put a hole in the top of cut-out Christmas cookies so they can hang from colorful ribbons. They look great hanging in each square of multi-paned windows.

Fresh Fruit Wreath
Edna Smith

1 straw wreath
fresh evergreen boughs
as many nails as you want fruit

ribbon for bow
fresh fruit of your choice

Pound the nails through the back side of straw wreath, so that nail ends stick out the front of the wreath about 1 to 1 1/2 inches. If you put them in at an angle, they hold better. Push apples, pears, oranges or whatever fruit you wish onto the nails. Fasten greenery in between fruit to cover wreath fully. Add a bow and enjoy!

Paper Chain Garland
Linda Mott

1" x 6" strips of red, white and green construction paper

Paste the ends of 1 strip together to form a ring, add more rings, forming a chain. Make it as long as you want.

Fireside Basket
Lena Romanoff

Find a large basket (can be old or discolored). Have the children gather bayberries, bittersweet berries, acorns, cones, mosses and other natural things. Cover the basket with the materials and glue in place. Set an artificial or abandoned nest on the inside and attach a small artificial bird. A wonderful winter time decoration!

Kissing Ball
Lena Romanoff

Find a large, round potato. Cut 3" sprigs of evergreens and stick them into the potato. You can use real or artificial mistletoe, rose hip bunches and holly leaves. (If using real mistletoe, keep out of reach of children, berries are poisonous.) The potato helps keep the greens fresh. A ribbon or chain can be suspended to hold the ball.

Gingham Check Bags
Pat Baer

Take tiny gingham check material and cross stitch initials or name, using the checks as the guide line for the "X's." You can then use grosgrain ribbon to make a drawstring or simply tie the bag, if using sachet or potpourri. The bags can be used as sachets, little jewelry bags or for many other uses.

Family Treasures
Leslie Deatrich

Each year, give your children a special gift in a frame. It might be an enlarged family photograph, a special piece of artwork from school, or a favorite poster. Write a message on the back of the framed piece before you wrap it. This way, when they grow up and leave home, they will have special family treasures to take with them.

Shine a spotlight at your front door and show off those beautiful holiday wreaths and decorations you've worked so hard to make!

Christmas Pomanders
Elizabeth Cassedy

2 large oranges
1 T. orris root powder

3 oz. whole cloves
1 T. cinnamon

Make a few holes in the orange, with a toothpick. Fill each one with a clove. (Children can use a toothpick to make it easier to push the cloves into the orange.) Mix together the orris powder and the cinnamon. When your orange is covered with cloves, roll it in the cinnamon mixture. Let your oranges cure for 4 weeks. To make it easier to hang your pomander, you can attach a ribbon with hot glue, or push a small paper clip into the end of the orange, leaving enough exposed to push a ribbon through.

Cinnamon Ornaments
Ginny Valley

1 1/2 c. cinnamon

1 c. applesauce

Mix ingredients and place on a piece of waxed paper. Spread the mixture out, and cut with a cookie cutter (small ones work best). Put a tiny hole at the top with a small straw. Put a ribbon through after the ornament has set.

Salt Dough Ornaments
Barbara Leonard

2 c. flour
1 c. water

1 c. salt

Mix all together, then knead. Use a little more flour for kneading, if necessary. Roll out dough to 1/2" thick (makes for stronger cookie cutouts especially when being made by children) and cut with cookie cutters or shape free-hand. Bake in lightly floured pans at 350 degrees for approximately 25 minutes, or until hardened. Paint with tempra colors and when dry, spray with shellac.

This recipe can also be used for making "playdough." After mixing dough, divide it into batches and color with different food colorings. Store in an airtight container. Great for keeping little hands busy during the holidays!

Christmas Pomegranates

Ann Mayse

Buy or collect different size pomegranates and allow to dry for 1 to 2 months. After they are dried, dip the whole fruit or just one side in gold or silver hobby paint. They can then be attached with wire to wreaths or hung as Christmas ornaments. This is fun to do with older children. The small pomegranates make beautiful decorations for feather trees. This craft can also be done with items such as pinecones, sweet gumballs, or miniature artichokes.

Spicy Gingerbread Ornaments

Debbie Clark

25 oz. jar applesauce
1 can (3 3/4 oz.) cinnamon
1/2 can (1 1/8 oz.) ground cloves

2 T. arrowroot
1/2 can (1 1/8 oz.) nutmeg

Pour applesauce into a sieve, over a bowl. Keep in a cool place. Drain for 2 to 3 days, stirring occasionally. Sprinkle a small amount of cinnamon over a smooth surface, as if sprinkling flour to knead bread. Add remaining cinnamon and other ingredients to applesauce, and mix. The mixture must be dry enough to roll out on cinnamon covered surface. Roll out to 1/4" thickness. Cut desired shapes with cookie cutters. Lift with spatula onto a flat surface. With a small straw, or sharp object, punch holes at the top for ribbon to go through when dry. With tip of knife, make indentations, not holes, for eyes, nose, and mouth. Cover with waxed paper and let dry for several days. Turn occasionally. Yield: 33 to 35 ornaments.

GiViNG...THE MEANiNG of CHRiStMAS

Soap Stars
Michele Roudebush

You will need a fresh bar of snowy-white soap and a standard cheese slicer. Wet the slicer and slice the soap lengthwise, making the slices about 1/4" thick. Lay the slice of soap on a flat work surface. Wet a star cookie cutter and press into the soap. Lift and gently remove the star from the cookie cutter. Return star to the flat work surface. With an awl or ice pick, punch a hole for string or ribbon to pass through. Red gingham is really festive looking. These stars are great for the tree, wreaths or even as guest soaps.

Country Gift Wrap
Diane Anderson

For a primitive, country Christmas gift wrap, stencil holiday designs on brown paper. A border of holly or santa and his sleigh add a wonderful homespun touch to your packages. It's a wonderful way to recycle those grocery bags. Top the presents with cinnamon sticks, berries, small bags of potpourri, or other country items.

Jeweled Ornaments
Marie Hale

A fun, holiday craft for your family is making jewel-like ornaments from stryrofoam balls. Using small pins, anchor beads and sequins into the styrofoam balls. This is great for manual dexterity, not to mention a quiet activity for a rainy day any time of year.

Gifts For Wildlife
Marie Hale

Collect pinecones from your yard or the woods. Spread them with peanut butter, roll them in birdseed, attach some colorful yarn and hang outside. For the squirrels, string peanuts, in the shell, to form a garland that can be hung outside. The birds and squirrels have a good meal, and the birds will gather the bits of yarn for nesting material.

Hang a wreath with big red bow on the bumper of your car!

Snowy-Look Candles

Lisa Murch

If you can't find the snowy-look candles in your area, make your own. Cover a round, snowball-shaped candle or a green pine tree candle, or any candle with whipped wax.

basic plain candle
tall 2 lb. coffee can
washing detergent powder
   (optional)
tongue depressor, fork or other applicator

egg beater
hot paraffin
cornstarch

Melt paraffin in coffee can over hot plate or burner. After paraffin has melted, add one tablespoon of cornstarch per pound of wax, so that wax will stick to the sides of the candle better. For added whiteness, add one tablespoon of powder washing detergent per pound of wax at anytime during the whipping. Start whipping the wax as soon as a skim forms on its surface. The faster the beater is turned, the fluffier the wax. When fluffy, daub the frothy wax with a fork, tongue depressor or gloved finger onto the candle.

Quick Dough Ornaments

Brenda Boyer

2 c. baking soda
1 1/4 c. water

1 c. corn starch

Combine all 3 ingredients and bring to a boil, stirring constantly. Mixture will magically turn into dough! Put on a plate and into the refrigerator to cool for a few minutes. Then, knead dough and roll 1/4" thick. Cut out your favorite shapes with cookie cutters. (Don't forget to put a hole in the top, so ornament can be hung later.) Let dry for 2 to 4 days. When dry, paint with stencil paint or any type of craft paint. Glue on sequins, glitter or whatever you wish. Put on a string or a ribbon and hang.

Calico Sachets
Karen Coll

Cut out rectangles of green calico material. Sew sides together and fill with dried pine needles, cedar branches, or balsam greens. Add a splash of pine-scented oil, if desired. Tie with ribbon and use for scenting drawers or closets.

Birch Log Centerpiece
Karen Coll

Take a white birch log, approximately 18", and drill 2 holes in the center, 6" apart. Choose candles of desired size and use to measure holes. Place candles in log and decorate base with fresh evergreens and pinecones for a lovely centerpiece.

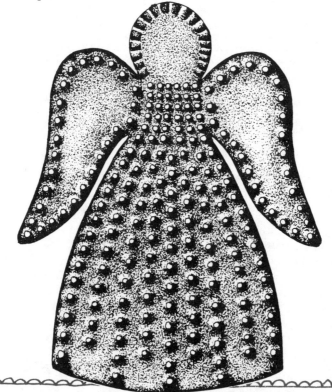

Bring out all your very best quilts and layer in chairs, couches, fold on top of cupboards—make your home cozy for the holidays!

Spicy Potpourri

Lisa Prichard

1/2 c. dried apples, cut in pieces
4 cinnamon sticks, broken into pieces
1 whole nutmeg, broken into pieces
2 T. whole allspice

1/2 c. whole cranberries, dried
2 T. whole cloves

Mix up a batch and attach a small bag of potpourri to Christmas gifts for family and friends.

Herbal Wreath

Joyce Newburn

Make an herbal wreath straight from your own garden. Take a straw base and attach thyme, rosemary, marjoram, basil, sage and as many more herbs as you like. A fat candle in the center adds the finishing touch. Wreath must be placed on a tray and watered each day to keep herbs looking nice, and to make it last through the holidays.

Apple Ring Ornaments

Laurie Keep

When using apple rings for ornaments on your country tree, use a star or heart cookie cutter to punch out the middle of the ring. You will get 2 ornaments from one slice, the cut-out and the ring with the cut-out design!

Gift Bags

Debbie Clement

Take a brown paper lunch bag and stamp it with designs using Christmas rubber stamps. Fill the bags with goodies, tie with ribbon and distribute to mail, trash and newspaper people as a thank you and a Christmas greeting.

Holiday Potpourri

Tessa Adelman

On a winter day, stroll through the woods to gather pinecones and cedar. Add holly berries, place in a bowl and enjoy!

GIViNG...THE MEANING of CHRiSTMAS

Cranberry Centerpiece

Anne Cartwright

Using a vase-size brandy snifter, center a candle inside. The candle should be approximately 3" in diameter and 2/3 the height of the snifter. Fill the container with fresh whole cranberries, leaving approximately 1/3 of the candle exposed. Tie a Christmas ribbon around the stem, making a pretty bow. Add some fresh-cut greens for the smell of the holidays. A vanilla or green candle keeps the colors of the season.

Christmas Luminaries
Mimi Shanahan

A fun idea for Christmas is to get together with some neighbors and friends and make Christmas luminaries. Buy brown paper lunch bags (everyone decides how many they want to make) and some stenciling material. Any stencil designs can be used. Kitty litter can be used instead of sand. These bags can be carefully folded and used for several years.

> *Videotape family members and loved ones during the holidays . . . telling stories, singing songs, recalling the "olden" days! These are our best Christmas keepsakes.*

Cookie Dough Ornaments

Sandy Jean Tucker

4 c. all purpose flour
1/4 c. cinnamon
1 1/2 c. lukewarm water

1 c. salt
3 T. nutmeg
2 T. ground cloves

Sift dry ingredients together. Add water until dough is the consistency of molding clay. Dough can be wrapped and refrigerated overnight. Shape the dough with cookie cutters or free-hand designs of your choice. Bake in a pre-heated 300 degree oven for 1 hour. Brush with polyurethane once your "cookies" are cool.

Hors D'Oeuvres Christmas Tree

Patricia Loughren

Start with a styrofoam cone (10" tall) to make an edible hors d'oeuvres Christmas tree/centerpiece. First cover the "tree" with romaine lettuce leaves to make it green. Using toothpicks, add olives, cherry tomatoes, chunks of cheese and cauliflower florets. These are the "ornaments." A thick piece of cheese, cut in the shape of a star, tops the tree.

Dogwood Blossom Decorations

Rebecca Ilgen

When the Dogwood is in full bloom, harvest the blossoms. Dry them in silica gel in the microwave, and store away in airtight containers until Christmas. The white blossoms are a perfect holiday decoration not only on the Christmas tree, but on greenery and added to pinecone arrangements. Dried Queen Anne's Lace is a beautiful decoration for your tree as well, giving the appearance of laced snowflakes. Enjoy them anywhere and everywhere!

Carve out apples, oranges and artichokes and tuck in votive candles. Candles everywhere say "welcome."

45

GiViNG...THE MEANiNG of CHRiS†MAS

Recycled Holiday Greens   *Lynda Martino*

After the holidays, you may want to recycle your wreaths, garlands and
even your Christmas tree into a wonderful potpourri. It's great for your
spirits as well as the environment! Allow your greenery to dry thoroughly
by hanging it upside down in a warm (but not too hot) location. All types
of evergreens may be used . . . boxwood, coned cedar, incense cedar,
juniper, noble fir, balsam fir (very fragrant), etc. Use garden clippers to
cut them into two to three inch pieces. In a very large ceramic or glass
bowl assemble together with five or six cups of the greenery mixture any
number or all of the following ingredients in 1/2 cup amounts:

> **Small cinnamon sticks broken into pieces**
> **Whole cloves**
> **Whole allspice**
> **Nutmeg (crushed open to add texture & release their full
>   fragrance)**
> **Bay leaves (whole and broken pieces)**
> **Star anise**
> **Small or medium size pinecones**
> **Orange, lemon or lime slices (cut very thin and allowed to
>   fully dry)**
> **Orange, lemon or lime peel**
> **Holly and juniper berries**
> **Lemon verbena or lemon balm leaves**

This mixture will smell wonderful as is but will be even more fragrant if
you add essential oil and a fixative. Depending on the oil you choose, you
can create either a Christmas potpourri or a kitchen potpourri. Four to six
drops of balsam fir oil will bring out the greenery aroma thus creating a
Christmas fragrance; a spicy or citrus oil will make a wonderful kitchen
scent. A fixative such as oak moss or orris root chips (or orris root powder; 1 T.) will make your fragrance last much longer. After you have
carefully blended together all your ingredients with a wooden spoon, store
your potpourri in an airtight glass or ceramic container and keep in a dark
location for a minimum of six weeks. If you can wait eight to twelve
weeks, so much the better. During this "curing" time be sure to shake or
stir the potpourri a couple times a week. Once your potpourri is ready to
be set out, "garnish" it with items such as star anise, pinecones, small
pomegranates, miniature artichokes, etc. Use your imagination to create
your own signature-style potpourri!

Christmas Tree "Snow"   *Lynda Martino*

This is my mother's recipe for "snow" on a Christmas tree. All of our trees when we were growing up had this special snow on them. My mother and I continue this family tradition each year with our snow-covered trees. I thought Mom was so clever to invent this idea, but she confessed the snow was featured on a popular TV show in the 50's called House Party.

To make your snow, pour about 1 1/2 cups of snowy detergent into a very large bowl. Put two quarts of softened or bottled water into a tea kettle and bring to a boil. Slowly add the boiling water to the detergent using either a hand-held or stationary mixer on the lowest speed until you begin to get a thick sudsy mixture. Continue mixing and adding the water until the snow gets stiffer and will almost stand in peaks. Switch to a higher speed to make it even fluffier. In all you will use between four to six cups of water and the mixture will more than double in size. This is why you must start with a large bowl. When the mixture is very fluffy, it is ready to be applied to your tree. Be sure to have your Christmas lights on the tree before applying the snow. Spread several layers of newspaper beneath the tree to catch any snow drops! Using rubber gloves on your hands and being very careful as the mixture will be quite warm, gently begin to apply the snow on the outer edges of the branches. The snow will look more realistic if applied in a draping-like fashion onto the ends of the branches. Try to let it drip off the ends of the branches for a very natural freshly-fallen snow effect. Allow your snow tree to dry overnight before hanging the rest of your ornaments.

This snowy tree, with a few white icicles and all white lights, makes a beautiful bedroom Christmas tree—very dreamy and romantic-looking. Use a white or lace tablecloth as your tree skirt. For under the tree, I complete the look with several white accessories—white on white gift packages, my favorite white teapots, white stuffed animals, etc. This snow can also be used on artificial trees, wreaths or garlands with the same beautiful results. After the holidays, simply pull off the larger chunks of snow and the rest can be easily rinsed off with warm water under the faucet in the bathtub or shower. Have a "snowy" little Christmas!

> *"At Christmas play and make good cheer,*
> *For Christmas comes but once a year." - Thomas Tusser*

GiViNG...THE MEANiNG of CHRiStMAS

Drying Fruits for Potpourri or Garlands
Lynda Martino

Oranges, lemons and limes can be sliced about 1/2 inch thick and set aside to dry on waxed paper, turning each slice at least once a day. Do not set them on metal surfaces or on newsprint. Setting them near a heat source and/or in the sunshine will help them dry a little faster. You can also place them in a warm oven (200 degrees) with the door open for six to eight hours but you will get the best color retention if you allow them to dry slowly and naturally.

Drying orange, lemon or lime peel—after peeling immediately tear into sections about 1 to 1 1/2 inches in size. These can be used to add wonderful fragrance and texture to potpourri. If you would like to use the peel in a garland, simply insert a toothpick into the peel until it is fully dried. After it has dried completely, gently push the peel off the toothpick. Depending on the size and thickness of the peel, it should be ready for potpourri or a garland in about a week to ten days.

Drying apple slices—wash and core an apple and cut into slices about 1/4 to 1/2 inch thick. While it is more difficult to slice them thin, it is worth the effort because they will look nicer and curl better. Immediately dip each slice into a bowl of water with two to three tablespoons of lemon juice added to it or a canning product to prevent discoloration. Set your slices on waxed paper turning once a day. Once dried, you can use them in a garland with other dried materials or string them onto some raffia for a dried apple wreath. They make lovely edible gifts. Six to eight large apples will make a wreath about seven to eight inches in diameter. I recommend Red Delicious or Granny Smith apples. If not eaten, your wreath will look good for about a year!

Fresh pomegranates will dry on their own if placed on a shelf at room temperature. Be sure they are not touching each other and allow for normal light and good air circulation. A pantry shelf is perfect. These will take quite a while to dry completely (two to three months) so try to plan accordingly.

Cranberries are also great to use in garlands and decorations but will only last one season. For this reason you should not use them in a garland or decoration that you plan to keep for several years.

The Spirit of Christmas!

Celebrating Traditions

ADVENT ~ TOY ~ CALENDAR
Open a door each of the 24 days before Christmas
and find a toy!

The Spirit of Christmas!

When I was a young girl on the farm back in the early 1900's, I remember most of all our Christmas Eve sleighride to church services. We loaded up the sleigh with all 9 of us and wrapped ourselves in blankets, wooly mittens and hats to stay warm, and sang Christmas carols the entire frosty ride into town. Two grand horses pulled the sleigh named Jeb and Goldie and I can remember their frosty cold breath in the night air. We always had snow for Christmas back in those days. Each year we would cut the top out of a tree on our farm for our "perfect" Christmas tree and trim it with clip-on candles (because we had no electricity in those days) and simple decorations. On Christmas morning we would light each and every candle (a big bucketful of water always stood nearby, just in case). Santa would come to our house on Christmas Eve after everyone had gone to bed. In the morning we would find a pencil, pad of goldenrod paper, a tangerine, 2 sticks of spearmint gum and chocolate drops on our plates; and if we were lucky, maybe dolls for the girls and ice skates for the boys would be under the tree. As poor as we were, mom always managed to put together the best Christmas dinner with chicken, mashed potatoes and gravy, homemade noodles, pies and cakes. We always felt as if we were rich because we had each other.

Loretta Nichols
Vickie's Mother
Gooseberry Patch

A loving gift for your child straight from the heart . . . assemble a recipe box with all grandma's and mom's favorite family recipes. Add new recipes each year along with funny little notes and sayings. A warm, wonderful gift to grow right along with your child . . . truly a box full of memories!

Celebrating Traditions

Instead of sending Christmas cards to people I see frequently, I add up what I would spend on cards and stamps and buy a gift for Toys For Tots or a local "giving tree." This also cuts down on tree destruction (paper products) and garbage, as most people throw cards away after the holidays. I give new friends a holiday phone call and explain my "cardlessness."

Donna Alongi

One of my favorite traditions is having my sister's three kids come over to make a Christmas gift for their parents. We've decorated a tablecloth one year with bubble paint and acrylic paint. Another year we painted Christmas balls. This year, either a table runner or placemats will be the project of the season.

I enjoy dressing up like a teddy bear and handing out toys with my favorite friends, who make me feel like a special friend all year long, THE FIREFIGHTERS OF MY TOWN. The kids really love getting the toys, especially the ones who come from scattered homes, no homes or that need special care.

JoAnne Trinca

We have moved fairly often with my husband's job and usually are away from family at holiday time, so we always buy tickets for our family to see "A Christmas Carol." The production varies from city to city, but the story remains the same familiar treat each year. It wouldn't be Christmas without a bit of Charles Dickens.

Joan Schaeffer

We like to make "Surprise Balls" for Christmas. Taking red, green and white crepe paper, and beginning with the best gift, wrap the gift with one color forming a ball. Continue changing colors and adding things that are of special interest to the child/adult. Our children love this because it can end up being the size of a golf ball or a basketball. Give teens a $5-$10 bill and younger children tickets to a movie or skating money, whatever fits the recipient.

Shirley Ainsworth

The Spirit of Christmas!

I love to give something good to eat to friends and family around the holidays. I like to make a large, homemade Cherry Turnover, enough for several people, and freeze it a few days before Christmas. I make a batch of simple sugar frosting and put it in small baby food jars, one for each turnover. On Christmas Eve or early Christmas morning, we love to deliver these in person with a short and quick "Merry Christmas!" We include directions to pop in the oven for 40 minutes and drizzle with icing to make a surprise snack for the family we have just visited. We have always been rewarded with a very surprised "thank-you" and many warm feelings when we leave. Well worth the effort it took. We remember never to stay and chat or accept an invitation to come in and join the family, because everyone's Christmas is special. We just give an old-fashioned Christmas wish and leave our edible gift. The thought and goodie will be well remembered for years. I "stole" this idea from a long-ago friend who always delivered ours on Christmas morning arriving in the middle of our gift opening, when I most needed a break from the small children's excitement! A most appreciated gift from the heart and kitchen of a friend. My friend is not alive anymore, but not a Christmas morning goes by that I don't keep an ear out for that little knock on our door.

Sharon Holmes

In Bavaria, people cut branches from flowering fruit trees (apple, pear, cherry) on St. Barbara's Day, December 4th. If they blossom by Christmas, the household will receive blessings.

Our church celebrates the holidays by picnicking together. We eat inside, but have grilled hot dogs, hamburgers (grilled outside), salads and beans. The teenagers organize the party, including the entertainment. We have the picnic on the Sunday nearest January 6th (Three Kings).

Mary Anne Perks

I come from a fairly large family of five children. We are all grown with families of our own and because of this, we have found it difficult for us to gather on Christmas Eve or Day to celebrate together. Two years ago my sister, Victoria and I came up with a party idea for December 23rd, which we lovingly refer to as our "Eve of Christmas Eve Party." We decorate my sister's country Cape Cod home and invite our family and closest friends to share the joy of the holidays. We listen to Christmas carols while the little ones open presents, we finish decorating the tree, and enjoy a variety of treats. We have started a family tradition which we hope will continue for many generations. Each year we anxiously plan and wait for the "Eve of Christmas Eve."

Jennifer Matzul

While your children are still young, make salt-dough ornaments using their favorite country-style cookie cutter shapes (hearts, gingerbread men). Put a wooden matchstick in the soft dough before baking (break off the red tip first) for a hole you can string yarn or brown twine through. My daughter and I made several dozen of these ornaments when she was small and we were living on a sailboat. Now that she's 25, living in another part of the country, and about to start her own family, they are my most treasured ornaments. Bringing back special memories every time I hang them on the tree.

C. A. Long

We have a Christmas workshop for the kids the first Saturday of December. Six or seven crafts are arranged for them to do and they spend about 20 to 30 minutes at each craft. We have a story time first, then do crafts, have lunch, sing carols and then go back and pick up the last of the crafts. Swags are always made for every family in the congregation. The dads always show up just in time to clean up the activities!

Netta Groat

For an ice ring embedded with fruit that won't dilute your holiday punchbowl, arrange cranberries, sliced oranges, lemons and limes and pour in a small amount of punch. Let freeze and repeat this process.

The Spirit of Christmas!

I worked with the youth in our parish for many years. One of the special things they did was to make centerpieces for the "Fall Tea." Then before Christmas or while we were caroling, they gave them to the shut-ins. This made the young people feel very special as well as the wonderful old-folks.

Marilyn Rokahr

At the end of every Christmas season, we save all the Christmas cards we receive, then next year, we cut off the picture (front of card) and use them for name tags on gifts. Also, we try to think up custom name tags instead of basic TO: Jessica; FROM: Mom & Dad. Some examples are: TO: The Loveliest Freshman at Plymouth North; FROM: The Proudest Parent in the World, or TO: The Star Baseball Player on the Plymouth Little League; FROM: Your Biggest Fan. It's fun to have one person at a time give out the gifts and read out loud the gift name tag.

Judi Campbell

We set up our Nativity scene using a small jewelry box for the manger, without the baby Jesus. We place a pile of straw next to it. When the children do good deeds like setting the table, picking up their toys, help-ing each other, then they get to put a piece of straw in the manger. By Christmas Eve the manger is well padded by good deeds and ready for baby Jesus' arrival on Christmas morning. The children are very proud of the part they play in making his bed comfortable.

Our neighbors get together the week before Christmas and go caroling in the neighborhood. We send out flyers letting people know they can join us or enjoy listening to us. We make copies of favorite Christmas carols and distribute them to each caroler. At each house we sing a carol followed by either "Jingle Bells" or "Rudolph The Red-Nosed Reindeer." These last two songs are well known by all the children, so they can sing along with us. We leave each house singing "We Wish You A Merry Christmas" and afterwards, we meet at a home for hot chocolate and cookies. All the children love this tradition. One year we were rained out, but the children wouldn't hear of canceling. We met at someone's house and sang to ourselves!

Sheryl Adams

When I was a child, I loved candy-coated milk chocolate candies or "a certain kind of candy," so Santa filled my whole stocking with just those! Children may have favorites that they would like delivered that way as well.

Martha Terrell

We have made a "Past Christmases" photo album to take along to Grandma's house for the holidays. We've gathered all our Christmas photos taken over the years, and put them in an album, in no certain order. It's fun to look at the pictures and guess the years they were taken and what happened special that year.

Melissa Hinte

One of our favorite family traditions is lining the sidewalk with "luminarias" on Christmas Eve. The candles inside these sand-filled bags are our birthday candles for Jesus. Before our children climb into bed that night, we all go outside and help blow out the "birthday" candles. Doing this has helped teach the children that the real meaning of Christmas isn't the presents or the decorations, but that it's the birth of Christ.

Kathy Hill

Did you grab the name of a homesick relative in your family grab this year? Send a little bit of home to them. Make a wreath of pinecones picked up in the woods. Send them food, pastries or candies made only in your state. Make sure to send items distributed in your state alone, and things unavailable to them that had been their favorites. If you don't know if "home state" stores are accessible to you, your department of tourism or commerce will be only too happy to assist you in your search.

According to the Irish, if you find a bird's nest in your Christmas tree, it is a sign of life and good fortune for the coming year. The first year my husband and I were married we were lucky enough to find such a bird's nest. We've kept it and place it in our tree each year.

Karen Roberts

"The ornament of a house is the friends who frequent it."
Emerson

The Spirit of Christmas!

My mom is in a nursing home only a mile from my house and I see her every day, but Christmas is very hard for most of the residents. Even if they get lots of attention, or get to go to relatives' homes for special times, they still want to be decorating and cooking themselves. The greatest loss for most of them is not being able to work and do things for others. My mom would rather give goodies and gifts than receive them. So, I give her goodies and little gifts in a basket to hand out to people who visit, to the residents she sees in the dining room and to the ones who work at the facility. This gives her that warm Christmas feeling she remembers.

The most important tradition we have is gathering around the family Bible on Christmas Eve, with the only light being candlelight, and reading the Christmas Story from Luke. So often, we get caught up in the commercial traditions and need to be reminded what Christmas really is. Luke 2:11 and 2:14 need to be read with emphasis—that says it all.

Lou Ann Freeman

We have a living, potted Conifer Tree that we use as our Christmas tree each year. It's about 5' tall now. We can decorate it in early December and undecorate it in January, and never have dry needles on the carpet.

Jeanne Traut

Each year, for our Christmas dinner table, we put a special favor at each person's place that they get to keep. Usually it's some sort of ornament for the tree that we have made.

When we were small children, on Christmas Eve, we would sing Christmas carols. My younger sister would play her "zither," I would play my "organ" (one that had numbers you followed to make a song) and my older sister would play her guitar. We thought we sounded great!

Jan Ertola

Do more of your shopping by mail. You can send delicious foods, gifts and even Christmas trees and wreaths with one easy phone call. Mail order companies will be glad to ship your gifts for you!

Celebrating Traditions

My favorite Christmas tradition was celebrating St. Nicholas Day, which falls on December 6th. On the night of the 5th, we'd hang our stockings up and go to bed. In the morning, we'd find tangerines, a St. Nick cookie and a piece of paper. The paper held a rhyme that was a clue to where our gift was hidden. You'd find your gift from St. Nick and tear open the wrapping. I can still "smell" those mornings—the tangerine peel, the nutmeg from the cookie and the excitement of opening the package. Mom was smart because December 25th seems a lifetime away when Thanksgiving is past, so having a little treat earlier helped with the anticipation and excitement of waiting.

St. Nicholas was said to leave gifts, candies and sweets on window sills, in shoes and even in stockings of good little children. Hearing of 3 unmarried daughters for a lack of dowries, he left 3 bags of gold. The daughters were married and the tradition of St. Nicholas began.

Teresa Labat

Call your local college or high school and find out names of international students who might like to share a holiday meal and your traditions. They are lonely for family and friends and need to see more of American life than the four walls of a dormitory room.

Do you know a retired person who might need a little extra income over the holidays? Pay them to bake your cookies, address your cards, wrap your gifts and save you time. If you're the person with extra time, advertise your holiday services.

Lynda Zimmer

The Spirit of Christmas!

One of our favorite traditions is bringing home the tree. For years we've gone to tree farms, carefully selecting and cutting our precious evergreen. Then we "recycle" the tree, at the request of the local lake. They place the tree in strategic areas of the lake to provide a nesting and growing harbor for aquatic wildlife.

Take time during the holidays to find the homes of shut-ins or live-alones and treat them to carols. If in a rural area, try to arrive in a horse drawn carriage/sleigh. Afterwards, all gather for spice cookies and hot mulled cider.

Don a homemade santa suit and wig and quietly jingle down the halls of a local hospital (get permission first of course). You'll benefit more than the receivers. The twinkle in your eye won't be mischief, it will be a tear of goodwill.

Cindy Wattenschaidt

After Christmas Eve church, we drive around our neighborhood and "ooh and aah" at the lights, while we sing our favorite carols. Then the kids leave little notes and snacks for Santa. While they're asleep, we leave crumbs on the hearth and the fireplace doors ajar. One year, I sneakily put out some crushed ice on the hearth Christmas morning.

On December 6th, feast of St. Nicholas, we put out my Dutch Grandpa's handcarved wooden shoes by the (inside) front door. We fill them with nuts and gold foil covered chocolate coins.

Eileen Clark

Invite a dozen friends over for a cookie exchange and have them each bring 3 dozen cookies packaged in 3's. Each guest will go home with 3 dozen cookies (12 different kinds). Share recipes and have a great time!

58

We always have a Christmas dinner with another family close to us and exchange gifts, but this year we are going to "adopt" a family and buy gifts for those people, who otherwise would not have such a merry Christmas.

During the week between Christmas and New Year's, our extended family rents a cabin at a state park nearby, and vacations together. This is our special way to celebrate.

Pam Bartholomew

I grew up in Wisconsin, the oldest of six children. There was a period in our childhood when finances were not in terrific shape. Because of this, we had to limit our Christmas budget. Instead of buying gifts for everyone, we drew names at Thanksgiving, while listening to our first Christmas carols of the season. After the Christmas Eve church service, we'd open gifts from our siblings. The giver had to write the receiver a poem, giving a subtle hint as to its contents. The poem was often amusing, sometimes taking weeks to compose. Some were written in haste, just before the gift was given. Each person opened their gift and read their poem, one a time, to savor the moment.

Sarah Austad

I cross stitch many small ornaments each year, date them and give them to friends and family who look forward to our "ornament of the year."

Patricia Loughren

The local garden club sponsors, "Christmas Tree Lane," a display of decorated trees by clubs or individuals. It is held on Thanksgiving weekend to get the Christmas spirit moving. This will be my 4th year as a participant and my theme will be "A Jewel of a Tree." Decorations will be handmade and purchased ornaments, earrings and such with faux precious stones. Last year my entry was "A Scherenschnitte Tree," using hand-cut Christmas ornaments, beeswax hearts and candles (from Gooseberry Patch), golden yarrow and other dried materials.

Elizabeth Heyman

The Spirit of Christmas!

For many years now, our family has been getting together at our home for a Christmas morning breakfast.

Grandma and Grandpa enjoy making popcorn balls and wrapping them in red and green paper for the holidays. All the grandchildren love them.

Sharon Hall
Gooseberry Patch

Every year, at the dinner table on Christmas, we use Christmas ornaments for place markers. I make the place markers by taking Christmas balls or bulbs (the ones that are glass, and are solid, bright colors) and using glue and glitter, write the family member's or guest's name on the ornament with stars or lines as additional decoration. After dinner, we place the ornaments on the tree.

Raylene Nunes

A new holiday tradition of mine is to buy a gift for a needy child or adult. For the past two years, I have bought a gift for an elderly woman, in the name of my great-grandmother who passed away. My hope is to make this "surrogate" grandmother feel as happy and loved as my own grandma Mabel.

I cannot get through the Christmas season without listening to Johnny Mathis' "Merry Christmas" album while wrapping gifts, and watching "How The Grinch Stole Christmas" and Charlie Brown and his pathetic Christmas tree.

Chris Serbia

Through the years, I've bought a number of Advent calendars. It's always fun to rotate them, so that they always seem new.

A favorite memory of growing up was Christmas Eve. My mother turned out all the lights in the house after it got dark. She only left the tree lights on. Then she lit candles all through the house. It's the most beautiful and enchanting thing I've ever seen. A tradition I continue in my own home.

Susan Smithee

My 20-year old daughter has always shared Christmas Eve with the reindeers. As a child before going to bed, she put out special cookies and hot cocoa for Santa, but she felt sorry for the reindeer. So we went to the kitchen and cut up fresh carrots and celery and she scattered them about the front yard, then went to bed with a sigh of relief. Thanks to her the reindeer would not go hungry that busy night.

Jan Kouzes

December 1st, I put a little stuffed elf (homemade or purchased) somewhere in the house. He watches to see who is naughty or nice. Each morning he is in a different place. Then on December 24th he disappears to report to Santa, not to be seen again until December 1st. My children are all grown now and still the elf watches.

Marlaine Pietrzak

My husband and I are with the Air Force. We are far from family members and close family friends. We make new friends at each new station (now in Charleston) and every Christmas season we host an open house. We invite all our friends over, the weekend before Christmas and serve a Wassail Bowl along with other traditional, and sometimes not so traditional foods. Since we are in the south now we serve southern fried chicken. We relax after the hustle and bustle of shopping and decorating, and just enjoy good friends and food.

Mildred Strobel

Our families and relatives are scattered in different states and across Canada, making Christmas with the relatives difficult. Several days before the holiday, we invite friends to come over for Christmas cheer and tell them to **bring the children.** Many comment that this is the only time the entire family is invited to an open house. They don't have to find babysitters and the kids all have fun with my own children.

Decorating sugar cookies is a family tradition. We set aside one night when everyone, even visitors, join in. We mainly do gingerbread men, creating everything from football players to self portraits. All with frosting and lots of imagination.

Sally Burke

The Spirit of Christmas!

Start a family tradition of reading aloud, "The Polar Express" by Chris Van Allsburg, on Christmas Eve. At its conclusion, give everyone a large jingle bell to wear. These can be easily made or can be purchased.

Donna Reynolds

We start the Christmas season with stocking hanging on St. Nicholas Day. Mold cookies and sugar walnuts are the traditional stuffing, along with one ornament for each child. For identification sake, give each child's ornament a different colored ribbon. It looks great on the tree and they grow up with their own collection clearly marked.

Maria Vaz Duarte

Each year we get together with a group of 10 to 12 friends for an evening of Christmas music, food, fun and what we refer to as our "ART-101" project. We pick a rather easy project that usually requires some simple cutting with a saw, minimal sanding, and some painting, yet does not require artistic talent. Some of our projects in the past have been little fleece covered sheep figures; Christmas geese cut out of plywood, painted and hung up with ribbon and evergreen; primitive santa figures for the hearth or mantle; Advent Christmas trees cut out of plywood and painted green, with little ornaments to hang on pegs representing the 24 days of Advent. These projects generally take 3 to 4 hours for two people to complete. This is truly a unique evening, full of fun and laughter. We combine a party with creativity and we often give these projects to those hard-to-buy-for people on our Christmas lists. We usually conclude the evening with coffee and a group photo and, of course, comparisons and teasing.

Joanne Martin-Robinson

We try to celebrate customs stemming from our ethnic backgrounds. Following Swedish custom, we put a bird's nest in our tree for good luck. I also use the Gooseberry Patch wooden cookie tree, but instead of hanging gingerbread men, I hang Swedish gingerbread gnomes. In honor of our German heritage, we celebrate St. Nicholas Day on December 6th, when the children put their shoes out overnight so St. Nicholas can leave them gifts, including the traditional bag of chocolate coins wrapped in gold foil. We also follow the custom of lighting an Advent wreath on the preceding 4 Sundays before Christmas. We gather greens and pinecones from the woods to make our wreath and then add the 4 candles. To remember our French ancestors, we serve a Buche de Noel for dessert on Christmas Eve.

Celebrate a theme Christmas. For our Williamsburg Christmas, we featured recipes from colonial days such as roast cornish hen, pecan pie, Yorkshire meat pie, syllabub and sack posset. The musical background was provided by tapes of colonial era music. The house was lit entirely by candlelight and featured decorations made with fruit, greens and nuts. A long swag of pine, studded with lemons and pineapples made a lovely centerpiece. We also made nutballs and trees, by hot gluing nuts and small pinecones to styrofoam balls and cones. These can be ornamented with canella berries or spray painted gold.

Suzanne Charland

My daughter, who is now 17, always had trouble understanding how many days before Santa comes. When she was about 3, we made a paper chain with 24 loops. At the top we put a special Christmas candy. Every morning she ran down to our family room, where the special Christmas chain hung, and tore on paper link off. When there was one left, she knew Santa was coming that very night, and she got her special Christmas candy to celebrate. Even when she got older and didn't believe in Santa anymore, it just wasn't the Christmas season without her special Christmas chain.

Faith-Mary Alaimo

During the holidays, treat someone to breakfast in bed! Fix a pretty tray with lacy napkin, fresh flower, morning newspaper, a pot of tea and fresh cranberry muffin.

The Spirit of Christmas!

About a week before Christmas, when school is out, we have a cookie decorating party. Both of my children, now 12 and 14, invite three or four friends. Using a butter cookie recipe and lots of different Christmas cookie cutters, we bake about 2 dozen cookies per person. We also decorate and personalize an apron for each guest. We buy inexpensive, plain aprons. We buy **tons** of sprinkles, tubes of icing, and colored sparkles. The kids get busy creating and lots of munching goes on! Milk and hot cider is served, and each guest leaves with a large red or green plastic plate filled with cookies. It's always a hit!

Patricia Donza

Our family makes a gingerbread house every year. This task started with a simple gingerbread house cookie cutter kit. Because the house can't be eaten until after Christmas, it's one if the last big projects of the season. The house is decorated, Christmas music plays endlessly, and there is lots of chatter and giggles. The project starts with making the house pieces, then the construction and finally the decoration. Piles of candy are lined up along the end of the table and each child gets a side to decorate. Mom and Dad stay close by for any needed consultation. Each year this project gets more and more elaborate. We are now cutting out our own pattens for the house, and last year along with a custom house, the girls made Santa and his sleigh, with eight reindeer. This year, who knows, maybe a town!

Lucille Festa

Every year we decorate the house, put up the tree, light the fire in the hearth, make scrumptious food, and invite friends and family over to help decorate the tree. It gives a great feeling of warmth and friendship.

Lorraine Athanosios

Because my sister-in-law cooks Christmas dinner each year, I have all of our family over for Christmas brunch. And because we have different religions represented in our family, we serve everything from omelettes, to bagels and lox, to pancakes, and all the trimmings!

Ann Glendenning

We put birthday candles in an almond braid coffee cake and sing "Happy Birthday" to Jesus on Christmas morning, before we open our gifts. We started this when our oldest was two years old, and we wanted a graphic way to show a toddler what we were really celebrating. We wanted him to have the right perspective about the season and the gifts.

Sally Betz

We always spent Christmas Eve with Aunt Bea. A sudden attack by the "flu bug" kept us all at home, leaving Mom unprepared for a Christmas Eve celebration. Dad was sent to the bakery for dessert, and returned with a beautifully decorated birthday cake. What better way to celebrate the birth of baby Jesus. Thirty-five years later we still have a birthday cake on Christmas Eve.

Vicki Iannelli

When we were getting ready for Christmas back in 1961, my 1 1/2 year old daughter kept asking, "When is Christmas?" Answering the repeated question was not enough. I decided to wrap some small gifts (starting on December 14 through December 24) and placed them on a wicker tree. As the presents were chosen each day, it was easier to see just how fast Christmas was coming. Now, 30 years, 4 girls and 2 sons-in-law later, the tradition still goes on. (Can't wait for grandchildren!) No matter what, this tradition has never been broken. Many of the gifts now come from Gooseberry Patch.

Lorraine Prignano

The Spirit of Christmas!

In our house, a family birthday entails a candlelight dinner and baby Jesus gets the same recognition. For Christmas Eve dessert, we serve an angel food cake with 1 candle, signifying baby Jesus' birth.

Anonymous

At church, I lead an Advent Workshop each year. We have a covered dish luncheon, a brief appropriate worship service, and then a 2 hour workshop period. For this, I prepare sample items and have materials available so everyone (children as well as adults) goes home with at least one new Christmas decoration. Our sharing fellowship time has become a new tradition.

As for family traditions, we exchange names, and fill a stocking for the name drawn. These are shared usually the day before Christmas.

Patricia Milliman

Every year since our first child was 3 years old, we had to keep our Christmas tree lights and all our outside (Christmas) lights on, so Santa could find our house. We have been doing this for 25 years. I still have two children at home, both in college, but we continue to do it out of habit. I really think they still like the magic!

Donna Guida

When I first went to work, I was single, and always had time to do things with my friends. We all made it a special point to get together the Sunday before Christmas to make cut-out cookies. As we married and had children, it became more difficult to find time to go out. We still make sure we get together for our annual Christmas cookie-making day, to catch up on all the news. After the cookies are made, the husbands and kids join us for pizza and, naturally, cookies for dessert. It is just our way of staying in touch.

Carol Serrett

Fill gift baskets with easy-to-make gifts of food from the Christmas kitchen. . .spiced nuts, herbal vinegars, jams and jellies, homemade pickles, nut breads and holiday cookies!

Last year, I had fun watching my 11 month old daughter's face when she came down in the morning and (WOW!), there was a Christmas tree, all decorated and lit, where a chair used to be. That was just the beginning of a magical Christmas season.

Heidi Schwarz Hosler

We started a new tradition (with the help of your wonderful catalog!) at school. We mixed up a batch of applesauce-cinnamon mixture. Then we cut out gingerbread boys (with the heart cut out), two for each child. We sandwiched the 2 gingerbread cut-outs together and put each child's picture in the heart. We used one school picture, face only, of each child. A straw was used to make a hole for the ribbon. The parents were thrilled with their gifts, the children loved making them, and we started a new tradition. It worked out so well, I did some for our tree, with our family pictures.

Suzanne Erbe

I have a picture, which my 7 year old grandson, Justin, drew and colored which says, "I Love To Make Cookies With My Grandma." We make cookies together during Thanksgiving holiday.

Shirley Lampky

One of my fondest memories of Christmas time when I was young, was that after our Christmas church pageant the kids would get a large bag of candy and a homemade ornament.

Kate Cody

After the presents are all opened, we sit down and enjoy a big breakfast, often fresh fruit, croissants and an egg casserole. A small gift box is at each plate, filled with small candies (usually foil wrapped chocolate coins). A bowl of rice pudding is passed and good luck is for the one who gets the hidden almond! It is then time to go to Grandma's house and celebrate.

Juliene Bramer

The Spirit of Christmas!

A basket filled with handmade Christmas ornaments is a special gift. Yearly made ornaments for close friends and family makes a very special tradition when used as gift package decoration.

Colleen Becker

Luckily, I had a tape recorder handy when it was suggested we all share a "special Christmas memory." We started with the youngest member of the family and ended with the oldest member, telling of their very own special memory. My husband and I found out about some wonderful times that our children remembered as special. (We had not realized how much they appreciated our efforts.) I also found out some very endearing things about my husband's Christmas in his home. Each member of our family will now remember the "special Christmas memory" Christmas.

On Thanksgiving, each member of the family brings his/her Christmas stocking to the family dinner. We then "draw" stockings; adults for adults, children for children. We set a limit on cost, but encourage home-made gifts. The stocking gifts are returned on Christmas Eve to be opened after dinner. It is fun to see the stockings hung in different families' homes during the Thanksgiving/Christmas holidays. Even Grandma and Grandpa are included, this cuts the cost down tremendously for fixed income folks, and they enjoy being part of the drawing.

In our nativity scene, we keep a fresh flower in the place of the infant Jesus until Christmas Eve at midnight. We place the infant in His rightful place on the 25th.

Pat Akers

68

Celebrating Traditions

We adopted a tradition used in my mother's family. When she was a small girl in Wauseon, Ohio, at the turn of the century, her parents continued the German custom of giving children their Christmas spending money on St. Nicholas Day, December 6th. We changed the custom slightly and gave each of our children a small gift to open on that day. It was something which helped them wait until Christmas Eve. Sometimes the gift was one from German relatives which arrived early in December, and just opening the gift made it very special indeed.

Kathleen Smith

When I set out my nativity scene, I leave out the baby Jesus. Then on Christmas morning my daughter loves to see that Jesus was "born" and is in His mother Mary's arms.

Rebecca Crowley

From the time my husband and I have had the family Christmas dinner (30 years +) we have always had a small, wrapped gift or favor for each member to open at the table, before dinner. It is a fun, together time, and everyone has a good feeling. It also makes the table look festive.

Marjorie Foland

We have a family tradition of reading aloud on Christmas Eve, "A Cup of Christmas Tea." This story is excellent reading during the holidays, and even captures the hearts of teens.

Cindy Meyer

I grew up on a farm, and the tradition I remember most, is that every Christmas my parent's brothers would go to the woods on my parent's estate, and cut our own Christmas tree. It was so much fun, and the aroma of Christmas time brings back that wonderful childhood memory.

Betsy Rose

Legend has it that burning a bayberry candle on Christmas Eve brings good luck throughout the New Year.

Judy Carter

The Spirit of Christmas!

Since her 9 grandchildren have gotten older, my mother takes them shopping on December 24th to choose their own gift and their 3 moms go along to help. Since we all live in the country or small towns, we go to a nearby town with malls. This is "kid's day," no serious shopping is allowed. They get to go wherever they want—some pick toys, some clothes, and some sports equipment. When everyone has his gift, we go home to oyster stew and date cake by the wood stove.

Sara Walker

Our animals, one cat and one dog, are our children, and are always included in our Christmas celebration. We hang stockings for each of them, which Santa fills with their favorite treats and toys. While my husband and I open our presents, our babies enjoy their goodies.

Susan Ferguson

Whenever we travel throughout the year, we buy souvenirs that will hang on our Christmas tree. Each year as we decorate the tree, the "ornaments" remind us of the places we have been throughout the years.

All year long, my husband takes pictures at work of fellow associates. We enclose the photos in our Christmas cards. Everyone seems to appreciate them.

Mary Ann Preston

When live trees became so expensive, we began a special bank called "the tree bank." Loose change (and even bills from grandmother) usually pay for our tree. We open the bank on Thanksgiving, and my 2 sons always did the counting when they were younger.

Another of our traditions is to put candles in all the windows after Thanksgiving dinner. Since we have 4 floors in our old home and lights in 24 windows, it makes for good exercise to ward off "turkey bloat." Our neighbors always expect the candles, and a tree outside, to be lit Thanksgiving evening.

Trudy Jo Snader

70

Celebrating Traditions

Every year, we focus on one country or region and incorporate elements of that culture into our holiday celebration. We like to include that culture's tree decorations, foods and drinks for Christmas gatherings, folklore and Christmas traditions/legends, costumes and language.

Rita Dow

Sherry Bolson *and her family also learn as much as they can about one particular nationality each year then celebrate the way they would during the holidays!*

For over 20 years, my parents managed a tree farm. My sister and brother and I would help plant seedlings each year (without much enthusiasm back then). For the past 10 years the trees have been harvested each year for Christmas trees. Each December we go out with Grandpa and pick out a special tree for our home. It was worth it after all!

Lauren Schnelle

Traditionally in Lithuanian and Polish homes, wisps of clean straw are placed beneath the top dinner cloth to commemorate the manger.

Alice Gudowski

Starting December 1st, we do something everyday for Christmas. This could sound overwhelming, but it is not. By telling the kids ahead of time that we are doing this, they want to know everyday, "What are we doing today?" Even shopping with the little ones is exciting when it is in the context of, "Today for our daily Christmas activity, we are going to buy a gift for Grandpa."

We act out the Christmas story on Christmas Eve. Older children can narrate, younger ones can act. We use a stick horse for the donkey, towels for the shepherds' heads, paper crowns for the wisemen, and gold garland for angel halos. It is so much fun and it makes a great video.

Gale Wightman

Take time out during the busy holiday season—go out to dinner with someone special or have a winter picnic by the fire!

The Spirit of Christmas!

We have many children (9) in our family, so we draw names for a secret Santa. Each child buys a gift (we set a $ amount) for their secret Santa. Not knowing who is buying for whom makes it alot of fun!

Barbara Oppasser

After being transferred a thousand miles from home and family, we faced our first Christmas alone. Knowing there must be other families in the same predicament, we made a list of those families, and assembled mesh baskets loaded with homemade bread, cookies and candy, for each one. We spent Christmas Day delivering them and needless to say, it was one of our most special Christmas memories.

Carol Meeske

To calm the little ones on Christmas Eve, my parents would serve peppermint sticks in our cocoa and let us open **one** gift. We usually chose one of the smaller ones, because "good things come in small packages." It made it a little easier to wait for Christmas morning.

Janis Wethington

I repair and dress old tossed aside dolls and stuffed toys to give to children where needed. Sometimes it's schools, sometimes it's church or a mission, different ones will ask for help for needy people. It's a good hobby and my "Christmas" is when the dolls and toys are picked up from my home. Until they are picked up, I keep them in a dollroom, where little girls will sometimes have milk and cookies, but I really think their mothers enjoy the visit most of all.

Laura Monroe

Celebrating Traditions

Each year my husband, Rick, and my daughter, Katie, bundle up in snow suits, meet friends at a nearby restaurant and have breakfast together. Afterwards we drive to a tree farm and cut down our Christmas tree. On the way home, we stop at a friend's house for hot chocolate and cookies. It is really a special day!

Sherry Thiesen

When our boys were small, we began a Christmas Eve tradition of reading two stories, "The Night Before Christmas" and "The Animals' Christmas Eve." While the stories were being read, we were recording it. At first, the stories were read to them and they talked about the stories. As they became old enough to read, they began reading the stories. Now it is fun for us to listen to the tapes and hear their voices change from year to year. And we have delightful sounds to go with our cherished memories. Our boys are now 17 and 14 years of age, and they still enjoy this tradition.

Janie Milum

For my family and I, Christmas is a time for remembering. Being married to a career Army officer, we have been a part of Christmas celebrations on three different continents, including a Muslim country. Of course this means we have never been "home" for Christmas, but we make home wherever we are stationed. As we unwrap our decorations, memories are always brought back as to where we were stationed when each ornament was purchased. And we remember the many friends we've made all over the world.

Peggy Crafton

*Another military family that collects ornaments of their special travels or events in their life is the **Nancy Pippin** family.*

Rather than being on the road Christmas Day, have a family party the Sunday before and ask everyone to bring an appetizer or dessert. You'll enjoy visiting, munching and exchanging gifts and have a much more relaxful holiday.

The Spirit of Christmas!

I like to give my immediate family members a "pre-Christmas" gift at Thanksgiving. I have a little bag of Christmas tree ornaments that I have made over the previous months. I like to hand them out and get everyone in the Christmas mood. I began doing this about eight years ago.

Jamie March

Christmas at our sheep ranch in Wyoming always includes garlands and red velvet bows on the gate down the road, a wreath on the sheep wagon door, clear blinking lights twinkling on the evergreen trees in the yard, Santa in the grandchildren's tree house and our pet sheep with bells on their collars, greeting holiday visitors.

Dianna Cosner

The day after Thanksgiving was devoted to making Christmas decorations for the tree. Our sons having school vacation and Dad having the day off, we were prepared with everything necessary for our theme, each year was a different one. With Christmas parades on television and hot spiced apple juice and crafty items, it was almost better than Christmas.

When I was growing up, Christmas Eve was the night my sisters, brother and I were "allowed" to open one package. My mom picked which one and (SURPRISE!), wonderful, warm flannel nightgowns for each of us to wear to bed that night. Perfect for pictures the next day. (Of course, my brother got PJ's!)

Karenlee Spencer

Marion Arcesi shares this tradition and gives her 4 children a special gift of nightwear every Christmas Eve. When her boys were young, Dorothy Hanford gave each of her children one package to open on Christmas Eve also—you guessed it, pajamas! Now their children and spouses eagerly await that one special package.

Something about Christmas that I have come to enjoy, is Mom's tradition of getting us together on New Year's morning. We all love the Rose Parade, so Mom makes a huge, beautiful breakfast to lure us back to the house. Following breakfast, while we're all taking in the parade, we dismantle the tree that we all gathered around on Christmas Eve. My two sisters and one brother are all grown, and it wasn't until I was all grown up that I truly appreciated this ritual. I knew it was a crafty way of Mom's to get help, but now it is a time of reconnection for us. We four siblings carefully wrap and stow not only our favorite remembered little treasures, but also our personal childhood memories that lie deep in our hearts. What was once a chore is now a lovely family gathering.

Alison Johnson

Each member of our family has a candlestick made to hold a very small red candle. They sit before our breakfast plates on Christmas morning, candles lit, while we have a silent moment (well, the kids try) counting our blessings. Then we make our wishes, blow out the candles, and dive into broiled grapefruit and Christmas-bread toast, so we can begin emptying our stockings.

Doris Hammer

We have a family night of decorating cookies. The whole family comes over one evening, on a Saturday, and I bake lots and lots of cookies. Be sure to take plenty of pictures. The little ones love it!

Rose Ayraud

> *The best way to clean cookie cutters is to carefully brush the crumbs away with a toothbrush. If you must use water, thoroughly blow dry with a hairdryer to prevent rusting. Never wash in the dishwasher or dry in an oven.*

The Spirit of Christmas!

Living so close to the beach, we take a harbor cruise to look at the homes and the boats that are so beautifully decorated with lights and wonderful animation. In sunny California, it's sometimes still 80 degrees even in December. But on our cruise at night it's cool, giving us a chance to wear winter coats.

Pre-school moms are always busy, seems we never have even 5 minutes to "calmly" talk. So during the holidays, I have all of the moms (usually around 15) over for a potluck and cookie exchange. With no kids and no husbands, we have time to talk and get to know each other. We all take turns sharing our own holiday traditions, a fun evening just for moms!

We make sure we send a card and current photo to our pediatrician and to the doctor who delivered our girls. We include a friendly note wishing their family a restful holiday, and telling them how much we appreciate them for taking care of our precious family throughout the year.

We adopt a family that is in need, either emotionally or financially, keeping it anonymous. Every day during the 12 days of Christmas, we send them a gift. The first day is 1 gift, the second day is 2, and so on. We enclose a little note with our gift, but we never sign the card. The gifts are not expensive; some note cards, a pretty dish towel, some food. We never tell them it was us. We feel great doing this as Christmas is a time to give, and we **all** are blessed by this tradition.

Debbie Morines

An old European custom— prickly holly in the house at Christmas meant that the husband would rule during the coming year; smooth holly meant that the wife would rule. Give it a try!

76

On Christmas morning we add an unexpected flair of international. We pass around a plate of fortune cookies and each person reads their fortune aloud. The fun, laughter and warmth of sharing is another of this season's blessings, a season which renews our sense of wonder, hope and joy.

Linda Kirchner

Years ago, finding that Christmas Eve and Christmas Day had become such a hectic, busy time centered around gift giving, we began a tradition we call "Little Christmas." Every year during the week before Christmas, our family and extended family gets together for "Little Christmas." We have an easy-to-prepare casual dinner (soup, stew, sandwiches). After dinner, we gather around the tree and fireplace for Christmas cookies and hot chocolate. The highlight of the evening is when each child/grandchild present shares a special song, poem, dance or story. Each "performance" is special and runs the gamut from a highly skilled piano piece to a toddler's twirling "dance." Grandpa reads the Christmas Story from Scripture, and Grandma reads the book, "Santa's Favorite Christmas Story." We end the evening singing Christmas carols. "Little Christmas" has become our very favorite Christmas tradition.

Helen McKinney

Some special gifts that you could give would be to have a musician arrive for a surprise serenade. Another is to have a story teller, dressed in costume, arrive and tell the children a special Christmas story.

Invite someone special to come share your Christmas. If they ask if they should bring anything, suggest they bring something that was traditional in their home.

Rowena Keaka

Instead of candy tied on the Advent calendar for our college-age, always-dieting daughter, I tie on diet crackers. It gets lots of laughs and a sincere thank-you from her.

Barbara Wilkes

> *To garnish your holiday punch, cut 1/4 inch slices from a green or red apple. Toss slices with lemon juice. Using a small heart or star cookie cutter, cut out center of slices and float on punch.*

The Spirit of Christmas!

My second son's birthday is November 28th. Traditionally at his party, we plant paperwhite Narcissus in cups, with white rocks. The kids all take them home as party favors, and by Christmas they have bloomed. So fragrant and fun!

Jo Carol Driver

On the day after Thanksgiving, Santa's Elf appears to watch over the Christmas activities. He sets in a high (beyond children's reach) centralized location, where he can observe the majority of household activities. Occasionally, he moves during the middle of the night or during a nap period to another location. His presence in our home and the home of my grandchildren has been very helpful in maintaining a degree of calm at a very stressful time. He travels back to the North Pole to report to Santa a few days before Christmas.

Helen Moor

Over the years (I'm in my 60's), I've collected santas. I now have enough to decorate one whole tree. We usually decorate another tree with the other ornaments. The "Santa" tree is a favorite of family and friends. We decorate the Santa tree early in December, and friends stop by bringing their grandchildren and other assorted "little people" to see the tree. They share a cup of cocoa, have a cookie or two and have lots of fun!

Pat Pettis

As a very young child I balked at going to Christmas Eve service because each year Santa would come while we were gone. If **only** they would let my older brother and me stay home so that I could see the real Santa.

Laurel Greif

My grandfather would always call us every Christmas morning at 5:30 or 6:00, say, "Merry Christmas!" and hang up. Now, it's a race to see who will be the first one to make the "Merry Christmas" call.

Every year, I try to pick a small craft of some kind to make together with my mom or a close friend, to use as package tie-ons. It's nice to sit together and talk about the holidays while doing something fun together.

Kimberly Burns

Every year, each of my three children select one old favorite cookie recipe and one new one for us to prepare. It's amazing how favorites change, and how they remember who "discovered" the new favorite.

Kathy Christianson

Starting on St. Nicholas Day, December 6th, I put up my childrens' stockings. Every morning when Matt and Megan awake, they check their stockings. If they were good the day before, they receive a small treat or gift. If they were not so good, they receive an onion. (The bigger the onion, the naughtier the child.) Needless to say, both are on their best behavior for the weeks before Christmas.

Katherine Wienberg

Christmas is especially hectic because of Christmas birthdays. My daughter's is December 24th and my husband's is the 25th. To simplify matters, Danielle opens her birthday gifts early on Christmas Eve morning and Gary opens his birthday gifts after Christmas dinner (5 P.M.) on the 25th. We have come to a compromise on birthday cakes. Every other year one "Christmas baby" gets to choose the type of birthday cake and blow out the candles on their day, the next year we switch. We have done this now for 19 years and it works well.

Connie Denue

A fire in the fireplace says "welcome." Keep several dry logs nearby for a quick country fire as well as a bucketful of cinnamon pinecones. The heat from the fire will scent the entire room with cinnamon.

The Spirit of Christmas!

For as long as I can remember, my family has invited everyone from our neighborhood and church community for a Christmas Eve get together. We spend the weeks before making cookies, fudge, and those great sausage ball biscuits for all the hungry folks who will come to our house. We have mulled cider and plenty of hot coffee available to warm everyone's spirit. We cap off the evening by attending our church's candle light Christmas Eve service. It's a great tradition that everyone seems to enjoy. Someday I hope to be able to take over the task from my mother, but right now I'll be content to be chief cookie maker.

Amy Gurtis

On Christmas Eve, before we decorate our tree, we have our "snack supper." We have chips and dip, egg rolls, crackers and cheese, tiny sandwiches, and meatballs with sweet and sour sauce. None of this can vary. One year I forgot the egg rolls, so we made a mad dash to the grocery store so we could have the traditional snack. We sit around the table and munch away and have loads of fun!

Barbara Loe

During the holiday season, I always like to have small gifts on hand for friends who drop by. One of my favorite gifts is to tuck a rice mix (Golden Pilaf Rice & Apple Almond Rice Mixes are found in the Kitchen Pantry section) into a decorative fabric bag. Our friends appreciate the thought as well as having something "special" on hand for a holiday meal. Be sure to include the preparation instructions with the mix.

Cindy Young

On the second week in December, before things get too hectic, I hold my annual cookie swap. I invite 25 friends who bake 10 dozen holiday cookies. We vote on the nicest looking cookie and even the saddest cookie. The winners get awards and we all have lots of laughs. All the women go home with a cookie cookbook that I have put together, with all the recipes for the cookies. My family eats alot of the cookies, but we also save some to put in pretty holiday tins that are given to people as little holiday remembrances.

One of the most important parts of the holiday season for us and our children, is sharing with the less fortunate. My husband had a wonderful idea when the children were very young and we have been doing this ever since. After the children make their list for Santa, they pick one of the gifts and give it to another child. We all go to the store and buy the gift together. We get the names of children and families from the school and from church. On Christmas Eve my husband and I wrap an empty box and place it under the tree. When the children open up the empty box on Christmas morning, they realize the small sacrifice they made to make some other child's Christmas a little merrier.

Barbara LeClair

We don't exchange gifts with my husband's brothers or sister, only with their children. So each year, I make up gift baskets to give them with jams and pickles or applebutter, whatever I canned that summer. I cut out Christmas fabric circles with pinking shears to fit the tops of the jars, tie with a piece of red or green curling ribbon, and put them in a basket with a Christmas linen napkin or piece of material to line it. I also add a craft, either a handpainted Christmas ornament, or even a painted wreath on tapered candles. I then add 2 or 3 kinds of "mini loaf" nut breads or homemade candy.

My favorite Christmas tradition was one I shared with my mother. Every year in the summer, we would go to the local county fairs and arts & crafts shows and buy each other a Christmas ornament. Then at Christmas time we would admire the decorated tree, and reminisce about the fun we had at this or that event as we looked at the ornaments. My mother died last year, but I am going to continue the tradition with my daughter when she is old enough.

Dena Cardi

The Spirit of Christmas!

We have a family decorating party for our tree. We serve cider, donuts, popcorn, play Christmas music and bring out our favorite simmering pot to fill our home with the smells of cinnamon. We watch the Christmas Story and many nativity videos to keep the holidays warm and wonderful AND on track. Christmas is a beautiful season of joy!

Shereelynn Koehler

As a child it was a family tradition to read "The Night Before Christmas" on Christmas Eve. After putting out a snack for Santa (and his reindeer too!), I would sit on my father's lap and he would read the story to me. A picture was always taken of this event. Now with our own children, the tradition continues. We photograph as well as video tape this very special moment. It is so nice to look back at Christmases past.

Jean Quinn

On Christmas Day we open only one present at a time. When we were kids it was fun because we could see what each person gave and received. Now that we're grown, it extends opening the presents for several hours, a nice time to gather with the family. Everyone can still see all the gifts and appreciate the thought put into the gift as well as fuss put into wrapping it.

When we were kids, and Christmas presents to each other consisted mainly of handmade items and small trinkets, we would open these gifts on Christmas Eve. That way, they weren't overshadowed by the "bigger" presents Santa brought.

Jeanne Itak

A delicious garnish for your holiday turkey or ham, here's an easy recipe for "Crystal Cranberries." Mix 3 cups cranberries and 2 cups sugar and bake in covered pan until berries can be pierced with a fork.

My mother always kept a Holiday Journal. It included a passage from each family member in which we reflected on the year in passing, and discussed our dreams for the New Year. She also listed all the Christmas presents we received, and a snapshot taken on Christmas morning each year. Now our Holiday Journal is a part of our family history and we only wish we had 5 copies. However, I have started my own journal.

Maureen George

Before Christmas Eve dinner, my grandmother (who was from the "Old Country") would place an old-fashioned wash basin in the kitchen sink. She would fill it with water and place a silver dollar (in place of soap) in the basin. Before sitting down to dinner, all of the adults and children would "wash" their hands with the silver dollar. This was to bring us prosperity and good fortune in the New Year. After everyone had washed their hands, the basin containing the water and silver dollar would then be set aside, and the first person awake on Christmas Day (usually one of the children) would go to the kitchen and claim the silver dollar.

We fill a medium sized punch bowl with hot apple cider. Then we make toast with hard-crusted bread and sprinkle with cinnamon and sugar. The bread is then floated in the hot apple cider. When the toast is soaked, it is removed and put on plates to eat. This will bring "good luck" in the New Year. We call it our "Christmas Morning 'Good Luck' Toast."

Anne Marie Gilmore

To deliver Christmas goodies (i.e. food, wine), my husband and I pick an evening to go caroling to our friends' homes. We give them a pleasant surprise and get to visit briefly during the busy holiday season. People tell us for months afterwards what a pleasant surprise it is to hear some-one caroling outside their house. When people find our "you missed the Howling Hoovers" card, they call disappointed to have missed us this year.

Colleen Hoover

The Spirit of Christmas!

Christmas Eve is always spent at my parents' home for the traditional Italian "Night of the Seven Fishes." Oysters, shrimp, crab salad, pasta, champagne punch, dessert and much more. Then, Santa and Mrs. Claus drive through my parents' neighborhood on a fire truck. Believe it or not, this has been a tradition for over 30 years.

One of my most beloved Christmas memories only works for a couple of years. After my children are in bed, my husband puts on his big work boots and steps onto a tray filled with talcum powder. He then makes footprints on the floor all around the fireplace, the presents, and the cookies and milk, to make it look like Santa has been there. You should have seen my son's face when he saw those footprints. He knew Santa had really been to his house. With 10 years between my two children, my older son now does the footprint honors for his little brother.

Mary Kelly

My husband and I have no children, so to make our tree decorating festive, we celebrate with champagne and special appetizers as we decorate.

Jennifer Clapp

Tuck away a small present on the Christmas tree for each member of the family. On the day that you take the tree down (at our house this is New Year's Day, during the Rose Parade) the whole family will want to help so they can find their present. It makes a depressing job a little more fun and adds something to the "helping hands."

For a very informal, easy and fun for all ages get-together at Christmas time, have a tacky Christmas tour. Invite families to meet at your house for delivered pizza and then go on a tour (caravan style) of the city to look at Christmas decorations (the tackier the better). Our local paper helps with this by printing a list of the houses and their location, but with a little research anyone can do this. Then afterwards you can meet at another house for dessert. Don't forget to sing Christmas carols in between houses.

This is an idea I plan to start this year. Starting in November I am going to pick one kind of ornament and make several of them. At the front door I plan to put a small Christmas tree and cover it with these decorations. Then everytime someone comes to visit during the holidays, I will send them home with a special remembrance for their tree.

Judy Butner

Being allergic to trees, we have to have an artificial one. Instead of going out in the woods for a tree, we go out to look for mistletoe. Once it is found, we take turns shooting it out of the tops of trees, then take it home and hang it.

Janet Salser

One of my favorite treasured childhood memories is of going to my grandparents' house on Christmas morning. My grandfather loved Christmas. He decorated the house with lights, put up the train track, and even had little cars to race around the train platform. When we were little, as we walked down the basement steps, much to our amazement, we would find Santa (Pop-Pop in his Santa suit) had fallen asleep sitting in his favorite chair. We would have great fun waking up Santa and having him give us our presents. Both of my grandparents are no longer with us, and it is with the same Christmas spirit that Pop-Pop had, that I lovingly put out my decorations, especially the nativity scene that belonged to them.

Michelle Lea Cione

The Spirit of Christmas!

In our family, we are all adults now so we have changed the way we celebrate Christmas. Since we all work and several are teachers who get out of school 4 days before Christmas, we had to limit the frenzy of Christmas shopping. It occurred to us that the most relaxed, fun and loving times seemed to be after Christmas, when the stress of "getting ready" was over. So we decided to achieve that "relaxed" feeling before Christmas. We tried drawing names, setting a dollar amount, and giving handmades; but nothing worked. So we decided to limit the gifts to books and **nothing else.** This has worked beautifully. Now with the frenzy of shopping for that special (and affordable) gift behind, we can cook, bake, and relax as a family, instead of trudging through the malls.

Margie Mitchell

We bake a cake, decorate it with a candle and along with our little girls, we sing "Happy Birthday" for the baby Jesus. This helps to remind us all of what Christmas is all about.

When names are exhanged in a family or a group of friends, keep them secret. And during the days before Christmas, leave little gifts and/or clues on your name's door, in their car, or leave a cryptic message on their answering machine. When getting together for the gift exchange, everyone tries to guess who their "Anonymous Santa" is.

Michael Gillett

Our concluding Christmas ritual occurs after the tree and decorations are put away—we make homemade vanilla ice cream! Using our leftover candy canes, we crush them and stir the candy into the ice cream just as it is finished. Of course we make a real family project of turning the crank on the ice cream maker. "No turn, no eat!"

My mother used to use leftover candy canes, crushed and added to tapioca pudding and served it on New Year's Eve.

Beth Krakowski

Five of us get together every December and have a cookie exchange. Last year, we decided to end the cookie exchange and have a country craft exchange instead. Since we are all "country" decorated people, we all share the same joy at receiving our exchange gifts. And the gifts last, the cookies don't.

Carol Wesoloski

We buy at least one new Christmas book a year. These are placed in baskets scattered throughout the living room. Every evening a story or chapter (Dickens' "A Christmas Carol" was last year's chapter book) is read. Few people can resist the illustrations and simple messages in our picture books.

Every year we buy one piece or more of Spode "Christmas Tree" china. We have enough now to set the dining room table to where it's a permanent decoration. How fun it is to have your morning coffee in a china Christmas cup and saucer throughout December.

Mrs. Joseph Stager

I really enjoy decorating using cut holly in stoneware crocks, candles everywhere and wassail warming on the stove. We usually have two parties and invite lots of friends to one; business associates to the other. I make plenty of cookies and freeze some too for drop-in company.

Dee Lakes

> *Visit an elderly friend during the holidays and make "tea for two." Bring along a basket of herbal teas and a plate of pretty heart-shaped cucumber & cream cheese sandwiches!*

The Spirit of Christmas!

I lived in Hanau, Germany while a child, and my most vivid memory aside from the Christkindl Mart in Nuremberg and the smell of gingerbread, was of an old city story. It is believed that at the stroke of midnight on Christmas the statue of the brothers Grimm (of **Grimm's Fairy Tales**) would change places. One brother is standing looking over the shoulders of his seated brother. How I wished to see this though it would have been a chilly trip downtown. The statue is located right in the middle of the downtown plaza, where on Sundays and Wednesdays there was a huge outdoor farmers market. Even in summer, I would find myself staring at these two brothers, who were born in Hanau. Today I read these fairy tales to my children and add some of the local lore I learned as a child.

Ann Cruzen

In early November our family gets together to make a list of people in our area who are needy, lonely or just kind of special for one reason or another. Several of our names belong to comfortable folks who are without family. Christmas is a lonely time without others to share it. All of these folks then comprise the current year's project list. I make stockings for each, decorate them, and buy goodies to fill according to their taste/needs. I usually sew little brass jingle bells to each toe. When I was a child our stockings had bells on them, so it is a happy thing to do for others. Then the stockings are divided up and assigned to a family member for delivery. The driver drops off each deliverer and his/her stocking at a sheltered spot. The deliverer carefully approaches the house without being seen, ties the stocking to the doorknob and rings the bell. Then they run to a hidden spot and watch from behind a fence or bush to be sure the person answers the door and finds the stocking. After they are sure all is well, they sneak secretly away and the driver later picks them up at a designated hidden spot.

Pat Henry

Be prepared ahead of time with gifts for friends who drop by during the holidays. Cups filled with gourmet coffees, teas, cocoas and gingerbread men; cookie cutters with your favorite Christmas cookie recipe attached; or handmade ornaments are all gifts from the heart.

Celebrating Traditions

I've been collecting santas for about four years now. My mother gave me my first santa and I've been adding to my collection ever since. I buy them at flea markets, antique stores, wherever I find one. I even have friends, across the country looking out for santas, so my collection is from all parts of the U.S. All my santas have their own room that they stay in until just before Christmas, when they like to scatter throughout the house!

Nanette Boyer

Lawrie Hamilton *also has a collection of santas which she says both cheers her and puts her in the Christmas mood.*

Our family's favorite Christmas story is entitled, "Why Christmas Trees Are Not Perfect," from **Gifts of Christmas, The Guideposts Family Christmas Book**. When you read it, you will know why. It still brings a tear to my eye after many, many readings.

Linda Kopisch

On New Year's Eve I serve my family roast pork. A pig always roots forward, symbolizing going into the new year, as opposed to a chicken which scratches backwards. On New Year's Day if the first person to enter our home is a male, we will have good luck throughout the coming year. Our "good luck" male is then rewarded with a silver coin.

Anne Legan

The Spirit of Christmas!

During the Christmas season of 1990, I had a Christmas ornament exchange, which I plan on doing again this year. I sent out invitations to family, neighbors, and old friends, all ladies. My invitation said they would share the Christmas spirit, meet new friends, and leave with a new ornament for their tree. I served coffee, tea, eggnog and lots of homemade cookies, muffins and pastries. Along with these I included fresh fruit, an eggnog dip, various cheeses and crackers. I decorated my house the old-fashioned way with greens, fruit, nuts, garlands of cinnamon sticks, bay leaves, and boxwood. Candlelight and a roaring fire added to the atmosphere. The different ornaments brought by each guest were all exchanged after we socialized and had our fill of refreshments. Many of my guests asked if they should either purchase or make a special ornament for this year's "event."

Brenda Brady

Getting together with friends and/or family was a tradition shared by many of our friends including **Barbara Riccetti.**

I started a tradition when my grandchildren were born. From their first Christmas until now, and I'll continue. I've made special Christmas ornaments, which are dated. Now they are teenagers and have started their own small Christmas tree with all of Granny's ornaments, and they call it "Granny's Tree." It makes me happy to know that they are enjoying them.

Mary Pellaton

Another special ornament tradition was collecting or making a special ornament for family members, children, and grandchildren. Some of our other friends who carry on this tradition include: **Mary Ann Young, Mindy Rynasko, Diane Robbins,** *and many, many more.*

The Christmas Groaning Board

Mulled Tea Bags
Joan Schaeffer

1/4 c. plus 1 1/2 T. loose tea leaves
4 (4") cinnamon sticks, broken into
    1" pieces
1 T. plus 1 t. grated orange rind, divided

32 whole cloves
32 whole allspice

Cut 16 squares, each 5 inches, of multi-ply cheesecloth. In the center of each square, place about 1 teaspoon tea leaves, 2 whole cloves, 2 whole allspice, 1 piece cinnamon stick and 1/4 teaspoon grated orange rind. Bring the four corners together and tie with string. Cover string with ribbon, if desired.

Tasty Chip Dip
Dale Palladino

8 oz. cream cheese
4 T. ketchup

4 T. french salad dressing
1/2 onion, finely chopped

Blend well then refrigerate. Serve. If you're skeptical about the ingredients, serve this dip at your next party or get together. All your friends will want the recipe!

Crab Dip
Alfreda Crosley

6 1/4 oz. can crab meat
8 oz. cream cheese
1 T. milk

2 T. chopped onion
1/2 t. horseradish
1/4 t. salt

Mix ingredients together and top with 1/3 cup almond slices. Bake in a casserole dish at 375 degrees for 15 to 30 minutes.

Grapes

Alfreda Crosley

8 oz. cream cheese
2 oz. bleu cheese
1 lb. seedless red grapes, washed
   and well drained

2 T. heavy cream
12 oz. walnuts, coarsely
   chopped

Combine cheeses in processor until smooth. Coat one end of grape with mixture and roll it in nuts to coat. Refrigerate.

Cheese-Do-Floppies

Alfreda Crosley

1/4 c. finely chopped onion
4 1/2 oz. parmesan cheese

2 c. mayonnaise
1 thin-sliced loaf of bread
   (square slices)

Mix onion, mayonnaise and cheese. Slightly freeze sandwich loaf, cut off crust, then cut into quarters. Spread with mixture and sprinkle with paprika. Place on cookie sheets and bake at 350 degrees for 10 minutes.

Spiced Tea

Donna Fawcett

1/2 gal. strong tea
whole cloves
1 pt. sweetened pineapple juice
sugar

1 qt. lemonade
2 T. powdered orange
   drink mix

Brew tea. While tea is simmering, add lemonade. Tie cloves in cheesecloth and simmer in brew for 10 minutes. Add pineapple juice and drink mix. Add sugar to taste, (it should be quite sweet). After it has simmered for 10 minutes, pour over orange and lemon slices in a punch bowl. Serve promptly. Serves 25 guests. The punch will be very hot, avoid cut glass.

A tray of red and green crudites for your holiday open house . . . green pepper rings, radish roses, broccoli florets, green onions, red pepper strips, cherry tomatoes, celery, pea pods and, of course, yummy dill or spinach dip!

Ham and Swiss Rolls

Charmaine Hahl

1 lb. baked ham, ground
4 T. dijon style mustard
1 medium onion, peeled and minced
2 sticks butter or margarine, melted
4 pkg. (2 doz. each) small finger rolls

4 oz. swiss cheese, grated
2 T. poppy seed
1 T. worcestershire sauce

Mix all ingredients until well blended. Using a serrated knife, slice an entire package of rolls in half, horizontally. Spread the bottom half with 1/4 of the ham mixture, replace the top half. Put the rolls back in the foil package, wrap with plastic wrap and then with freezer wrap, and seal tightly. Label and date. Repeat with remainder of rolls. When ready to serve, remove from freezer. Preheat oven to 325 degrees and bake rolls for approximately 20 to 30 minutes, until hot through. To use ham mixture as a spread with crackers and fresh vegetables, use only 1 stick of butter or margarine and several tablespoons of beef broth, enough to bring it to the proper consistency.

This recipe was found in a cookbook by Mary Reynolds Smith, and quickly became a favorite at our home many years ago. It's easy to fix, can be made ahead of time and frozen until needed. Another plus, it can be mounded on a platter and surrounded by crackers and crudites. It's a great recipe to have in these hectic times! As an added bonus, you could give a tray of these to a friend and know the happiness of having shared something of yourself. Which is after all, the essence of "giving."

Mushroom Appetizer Squares

1-8 oz. can refrigerated
   crescent rolls
2 c. mushroom slices
1/4 c. margarine, melted

1/2 c. (2 oz.) monterey
   jack cheese
1/2 t. oregano leaves
1/4 t. onion salt

Separate dough into 2 long rectangles. Press onto bottom and 1/2 inch high around sides of 13" x 9" pan. Toss mushrooms with margarine; arrange on dough. Sprinkle with cheese and seasonings. Bake at 375 degrees, 20-25 minutes. Cut into squares. Serve warm. Makes 2 dozen.

Crabbies
Louise Churchill

1 small can deveined shrimp
1 jar sharp pasteurized processed
    cheese spread
1/4 t. salt

1 T. mayonnaise
1 stick maragrine
6 english muffins
1/4 t. garlic salt

Beat cheese, margarine and mayonnaise until smooth. Crumble shrimp into mixture. Beat in salt and garlic salt. Cut english muffins into quarters and spread mixture generously on them. Put under broiler and cook until lightly brown. Serve hot. Makes 48.

Herbed Popcorn
Judy Carter

1 lb. butter, melted
garlic salt, to taste
popped corn

2 t. marjoram
2 t. sweet basil

Mix herbs and garlic salt and add to melted butter. Pour over popcorn.

Debbie's Long-Distance Michigan Corn Chip Dip
Dawn Marshall

32 oz. sour cream
1 t. seasoned salt
6 green onions
8 oz. colby or mild cheddar cheese

16 oz. cream cheese
1 large tomato
1 can large olives, pitted
    and drained

Soften cream cheese and beat until fluffy. Add sour cream and mix thoroughly. Add the salt; taste it. So far, so good. Cut the tomato into small pieces. Do the same with the onion, but make the onion pieces smaller than the tomato pieces. Slice the olives, into pieces smaller than the tomato, but bigger than the onion. Mix the sour cream mixture with the tomato mixture. Pour into a 13" x 9" x 2" dish. Then grate cheese on top of the dip mixture. Garnish with parsley, paprika and green onions. Serve with corn chips, vegetables, dip-size chips, round buttery-flavored crackers or whatever you like.

THE CHRISTMAS GROANING BOARD

Spicy Cheese Ball

Susan Andrews

1 1/2 lb. sharp cheddar
4 small pkgs. cream cheese
1 lb. toasted peanuts
    (crushed with rolling pin)

2 to 3 T. chili powder
4 pimento peppers
8 buttons garlic, minced
mayonnaise

Grate cheese. Mix cream cheese, cheddar, garlic and peppers. Add chili powder. Salt and pepper to taste. Add 3/4 of crushed peanuts. Mix with enough mayonnaise to mold. Use your hands to shape into a ball. Roll in remainder of crushed peanuts. Dust with chili powder. Refrigerate.

Bean Dip

Debbie Meyer

2 cans chili beef soup
7 oz. chili salsa (medium-hot)
1 small can black olives, sliced

1 lb. cheddar cheese, grated
1 medium red onion,
    chopped

Mix all ingredients. Bake at 300 degrees for 30 minutes. When serving keep hot in a crockpot and serve with tortilla chips.

Punch

Alice Gudowski

1/2 c. lemon juice
1 c. cranberry juice
1 c. strong tea
1 (25.6 oz.) bottle white rum

1/4 c. sugar
1 c. orange juice
1 doz. cloves

Mix all ingredients together in a punch bowl. Let stand in refrigerator for 1 hour. Add ice cubes and decorate with lemon slices.

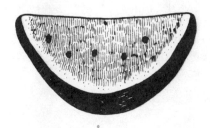

Holiday ✭ Open ✭ House

Angels on Horseback

Debbie Clement

3 doz. oysters
18 slices thin bacon
2 T. parsley, chopped

1 t. paprika
salt and pepper
6 lemon wedges

Cut bacon in half; place oyster in center. Sprinkle with seasonings and parsley. Wrap bacon around oyster and secure with pick. Place on rack in shallow pan. Bake at 450 degrees for 6 to 8 minutes or until bacon is crisp. Serve hot with lemon.

Grapefruit Slush

Ruth Fabian

1 medium can grapefruit sections
1 c. water

1/2 c. honey

Boil all the ingredients for 5 minutes. Cool and freeze in serving dishes or plastic containers. Remove from freezer 15 minutes before serving and scoop into sherbet dishes. Pour ginger ale over all and serve.

Swedish Cream

Ruth Fabian

2 c. whipping cream
1 envelope gelatin
1 pt. sour cream

1 c. sugar
1 t. vanilla

Soften gelatin in 1/2 cup of water. Heat to warm the whipping cream, sugar and gelatin, stirring constantly. Cool mixture until slightly thickened. When cool and thick, use a wire whip to fold in vanilla and sour cream. Refrigerate. Serve in small dishes with raspberries or other fruit.

The Christmas Groaning Board

Garlic Spread

Susan Smithee

1 large pkg. cream cheese
   (room temperature)
chopped nuts (optional)

milk
garlic powder, to taste

Mix all ingredients together, adding enough milk to make an easy spread of the cheese. Serve with crackers, as a dip, or make finger sandwiches. The garlic is what makes this dip, so do not use it too sparingly.

Sonia's Holiday Sangria

Sonia Bracamonte

6 oz. can strawberry nectar
small can frozen orange juice
1/2 qt. carbonated citrus beverage
fresh fruit (approx. 1 c. , diced)

6 oz. can peach nectar
dash of cinnamon
1 qt. hearty burgandy
   wine

Use whatever fresh fruit is in season. Combine all ingredients in a large container, adding fruit last, to float on top. Cover and let stand. Refrigerate for 24 hours, allowing flavors to mingle. Serve chilled. Makes 1 punch bowl.

Mexican Ole!

3 medium soft avocados
2 T. lemon juice
1/2 t. salt
1/4 t. pepper
1 c. sour cream
1/2 c. mayonnaise
1 pkg. taco seasoning
2 cans plain bean dip

1 bunch green onions
   with tops, chopped
2-3 medium tomatoes
   cored and chopped
6 oz. pitted ripe olives,
   chopped
8 oz. shredded cheddar
1 pkg. round tortilla
   chips

Peel, pit and mash avocados with lemon juice. Combine sour cream, mayonnaise and taco seasoning in a separate bowl. Spread bean dip on bottom of a 11" x 7" (or 9" x 13") pan. Top with avocado mixture, then sour cream mixture. Sprinkle with onions, tomatoes and olives. Cover with cheese. Serve room temperature or chilled with a big bowl of tortilla chips for dipping--ole!

Patrick's Holiday Egg Nog
Teresa Labat

6 egg yolks
6 egg whites
1/2 pt. whipped cream
1 c. milk OR 1/2 c. each bourbon
    and rum

1/2 c. sugar
1/4 t. salt
2 c. milk

Beat egg yolks slightly. Add sugar and heat until thick and lemony looking. At low speed, add the milk or bourbon and rum. Chill for several hours. Beat egg whites and salt together. Whip the cream until stiff. Stir milk into the chilled yolk mixture. Fold in whipped egg whites and then the whipped cream. Chill for 1 hour. Stir before serving. Sprinkle with nutmeg. Makes 15-5 oz. servings.

Spiced Percolator Punch
Cheryl Parker

Percolator punch is great to make during the holidays and all winter too. It makes the house smell great.

2-32 oz. cranberry juice
46 oz. can pineapple juice
    (unsweetened)
peel from 1/4 orange, cut in strips

1 c. brown sugar
4 t. whole cloves
12" cinnamon stick,
    broken

Mix together the juices and the brown sugar. Put liquid into a large (24 cup) percolator coffee pot. Put the cloves, cinnamon stick and orange peel into the basket, and perk. Add 1/5 of light rum if desired. Makes 17 cups.

Hot Cranberry Punch
Mabel Lamb

2-32oz. low calorie cranberry
    juice cocktail
6 oz. can pineapple or orange
    juice concentrate

2 c. water
12" cinnamon sticks
3 whole cloves

Heat to hot, then simmer for 20 minutes

The Christmas Groaning Board

Holiday Mulled Punch

Nancie Gensler

3/4 c. brown sugar
1/4 t. salt
1/2 t. cloves
1/4 t. nutmeg
2 cans cranberry sauce (jelly)
4 c. pineapple juice, unsweetened

1 c. water
1/2 t. cinnamon
1/4 t. allspice
additional 3 c. water

Combine brown sugar, 1 cup water, salt, cinnamon, cloves, allspice and nutmeg and bring to a boil. Beat in cranberry sauce, pineapple juice and additional 3 cups of water. Simmer until heated through and all ingredients are well blended. Serve punch hot, in mugs with a cinnamon stick and a smidge of butter or margarine. You can add red wine or bourbon to make this an excellent "heady" brew.

Peppermint Hot Chocolate

Rowena Keaka

hot chocolate
peppermint tea bag

1 oz. peppermint schnapps

Pour hot chocolate over a peppermint tea bag, let steep. If you want more peppermint zing, add peppermint schnapps.

Hot Pilgrim

1-gallon cranberry juice
2 oranges, thickly sliced,
    quartered, seeded
    (8 slices approx.)

20 cinnamon sticks
    (retain 16 for
    garnish)
8 whole cloves

Heat to boiling and simmer for 2 minutes. Serve in 8-ounce earthenware cups or mugs. Decorate each with cinnamon stick. Serves 16.

Holiday Spread
Beverly McKay

2-16 oz. cream cheese
1 jar cocktail sauce

parsley
fresh or frozen salad shrimp

Soften cream cheese and cook shrimp. Shape cream cheese into any Christmas shape (tree, bell, etc.) and let harden. Pour cocktail sauce over top and cover with shrimp. Sprinkle parsley around and surround with crackers of your choice.

Chocolate Coffee
Betty Sack

1/2 c. instant coffee
1 1/2 c. powdered creamer
1/2 c. chocolate-flavored powdered
    drink mix

1/4 c. sugar
dash of salt
1/2 t. nutmeg

Mix ingredients together in a blender. Add to cup of hot water according to taste.

Hot Buttered Rum
Betty Sack

1 qt. vanilla ice cream
1 lb. brown sugar
2 t. cinnamon

1 lb. powdered sugar
1 lb. butter, softened
1 to 2 t. nutmeg

Combine ingredients and store in freezer. To serve combine: 1 shot rum, 2/3 c. boiling water, and 4 tablespoons butter; stirring well.

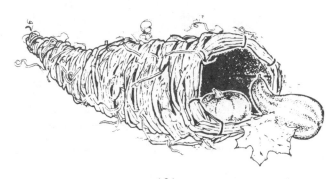

The Christmas Groaning Board

Festive Eggnog Punch
Caren Schulze

1 qt. eggnog
2 pt. peppermint ice cream, softened

1 c. ginger ale

Blend ingredients together. Pour into a punch bowl. Hang small candy canes around bowl.

Cheese Spread
Barbara Heck

3-8 oz. pkgs. cream cheese
1 medium green pepper
3 medium carrots
3 to 4 stalks celery
10 to 12 radishes

1 medium cucumber
1 medium red onion
1 T. garlic salt
dash of salt

Chop all ingredients, except cream cheese, in blender with a small amount of water. Drain and squeeze out excess water. Mix with cheese. Let sit overnight in refrigerator. Serve with crackers or veggies.

Hot Spiced Wine Punch
Barbara Heck

1 qt. apple juice
1 qt. cranberry juice
1/2 c. lemon juice
2 qt. rose wine
peel of 1 lemon, cut in strips

2 c. sugar
4 cinnamon sticks
12 whole cloves
1 qt. water

Combine cranberry and apple juices, water, sugar, cinnamon sticks, cloves and lemon peel in a pan. Bring to a boil. Stir in sugar until dissolved. Simmer uncovered for 15 minutes. Add wine and lemon juice. Heat, but do not boil. Serve in punch bowl. Garnish with lemon slices. Serves 40. BE SURE PUNCH BOWL IS CAPABLE OF HOLDING HOT PUNCH.

Keep camera handy during the holidays—snap pictures of kids with cookie faces, rosy cheeks & happy smiles!

Russian Tea
Jacqueline Cline

16 c. water
whole cloves (enough to fill a
    tea steeper)
4 small cans frozen orange juice
6 small tea bags

2 c. sugar
3 cinnamon sticks
1 large can pineapple juice
1 small can lemonade

Boil the water, sugar, cinnamon sticks and cloves on stove for about 5 minutes. Turn off stove. Add tea bags and steep for 5 minutes. Remove the bags. Add the juices and the lemonade. Serve hot from the stove. If storing left over tea, remove steeper of cloves and cinnamon sticks before placing in refrigerator.

Meatballs with Sweet and Sour Sauce
Barbara Loe

3 or 4 lb. ground beef
grape jelly

ketchup
non-stick vegetable spray

Use large baking sheets that have sides to catch the grease. Vegetable spray the pans well. Roll the ground beef into balls about the size of walnuts and place 2" apart on the sheets. Bake at 450 degrees until brown and done. Drain on paper towels. Keep warm. In a saucepan, heat equal amounts of ketchup and grape jelly until they are blended well. Use toothpicks to dip the meatballs into the sauce. Delicious with any meatball recipe.

The Christmas Groaning Board

Mocha Nog
Christine Pellicano

1 T. hot water
1 qt. dairy eggnog or 32 oz. can
1/2 c. chocolate flavored syrup

2 t. instant coffee
1/2 pt. whipping cream
ground nutmeg

In a large bowl, stir hot water and instant coffee together until dissolved. Stir in eggnog and chocolate syrup until well blended. Chill at least 2 hours. To blend flavors, just before serving whip the cream and fold into mixture. Sprinkle with nutmeg. Serves 6.

Cheese Ball
Donna Kincaid

8 oz. cream cheese
8 to 10 oz. soft cheddar cheese
1 to 2 t. worcestershire sauce

1 t. garlic salt
1 to 2 t. lemon juice
chopped nuts

Allow cream cheese and cheddar cheese to soften at room temperature. When softened, mix all ingredients, except chopped nuts together. Shape into a ball and then roll in the nuts. Refrigerate. Serve with crackers.

Shrimp & Crab Cheese Dip

1 lb. pasteurized process
    cheese spread
1 lb. unsalted butter

8 oz. crab
8 oz. popcorn shrimp

Heat in double boiler (I improvise and fill a pan with water and perch another pan on top) cheese and butter until melted. Add crab and shrimp, fresh or canned. Dip with pieces of french bread, bagels or crackers. Always a favorite at our family gatherings!

Hot Chocolate Mix

Edna Smith

25 oz. instant non-fat dry milk
16 oz. instant chocolate drink powder

1 lb. powdered sugar
6 oz. non-dairy creamer

Mix all together, fill a pretty container (coffee can or other can that you have covered with contact paper, painted, or covered with Christmas paper). When ready to use, place desired amount in cup and add hot water. For someone dieting, you can use sugar substitute for the powdered sugar.

Almond Pinecones

Laurie Keep

12 oz. cream cheese
1 1/4 c. whole almonds
5 pieces crisp, cooked bacon,
    crumbled

1/2 c. real mayonnaise
1/2 t. dill weed
1/8 t. pepper
1 t. green onion, finely
    chopped

Spread almonds, in a single layer, in a shallow pan. Bake at 300 degrees for 15 minutes, stirring often, until almonds begin to turn color. Combine cream cheese, and mayonnaise; mix well. Add bacon, onion, dill and pepper; mix well. Chill overnight. On a serving platter, form cheese mixture into shapes of 2 pinecones. Beginning at narrow end, press almonds at slight angle into the cheese mixture in rows. Continue overlapping rows until all cheese is covered. Garnish with artificial pine sprigs and serve with crackers.

Christmas Eve Sneaky Petes

46 oz. can pineapple juice
6 oz. can frozen orange juice
1 can pineapple nectar
1 c. bourbon or blended whiskey
    (optional)

6 oz. can frozen
    lemonade
1 c. apricot brandy
1 litre bottle lemon-
    lime carbonated drink

Mix and freeze all ingredients except lemon-lime carbonated drink. Put 2 large scoops in glass and add lemon-lime carbonated drink. Serves 10-12.

The Christmas Groaning Board

Wassail

Linda Crowley

1 gal. apple cider
1 qt. orange juice
1 c. lemon juice
1 large can pineapple juice

24 whole cloves
1 c. granulated sugar
4 sticks cinnamon

Combine all ingredients in a large pan. Simmer at least 10 minutes. Remove cinnamon and cloves. Serve hot. Makes a gallon and a half. Store in refrigerator when cool. Shake and heat a desired amount to be served.

Christmas 'MORN

The Christmas Groaning Board

Christmas Morn Casserole
Linda Crowley

6 eggs, slightly beaten
1 c. cheddar cheese, shredded
1 t. dry mustard
1 lb. pork sausage, browned
    and drained

1 c. biscuit baking mix
2 c. milk
1 t. oregano

Mix and pour into a 13" x 9" x 2" casserole dish. Cover and refrigerate overnight. Bake uncovered in preheated 350 degree oven for 1 hour. Serves approximately 10.

Favorki (Polish Sweet Pastry)
Jerrene Rogers

2 eggs
1 t. vanilla
2 t. melted butter, add whiskey or
    rum to taste

2 egg yolks
1 1/2 c. flour, sifted
powdered sugar

Beat eggs and egg yolks until light and fluffy. Add butter and vanilla and beat again. Add sifted flour gradually, beating after each addition. Turn onto floured board and knead to light elasticity. Allow dough to rest for 10 minutes. Roll dough as thin as it is possible to handle. Cut into strips; slit middle of strip and fold into create a bow. Fry in a deep fryer; place on brown paper. Sprinkle with powdered sugar.

Chocolate Chip Zucchini Bread
Jeanne Itak

1 1/2 c. all-purpose flour
2 c. unpeeled zucchini,
    finely shredded
2 t. lemon peel, finely shredded
3/4 c. cooking oil (vegetable)
2 c. packed brown sugar
1/2 c. walnuts, chopped
1 c. whole wheat flour

2 t. ground cinnamon
1/2 t. salt
1 t. baking soda
1/2 t. baking powder
3 eggs
1 t. vanilla
3/4 c. chocolate chips

Stir together flours, cinnamon, salt, baking soda and baking powder. In a large bowl, beat eggs, brown sugar and zucchini. Add oil, lemon peel and vanilla; mix until well blended. Stir in flour mixture. Gently fold in nuts and chips. Turn into 2 greased and floured pans. Bake at 350 degrees for about 50 minutes, or until wooden pick inserted in center comes out clean. Cool. Store in refrigerator overnight for easy slicing. Makes 2 loaves. Can be made in mini loaf pans if cooking time is adjusted.

Date Loaf
Donna Shadel

5 eggs
1 1/2 c. sugar
1 1/2 c. flour
2 c. English walnuts, chopped

3 t. baking powder
2 lb. dates, chopped

Beat eggs and add sugar. Sift flour and baking powder together and add to egg mixture. Mix in dates and walnuts. Put into 2, greased and floured, small loaf pans. Bake at 325 degrees until toothpick shows that it is done. It is best if it is made a week or two ahead of time, then wrapped in foil and refrigerated to let it season.

The Christmas Groaning Board

Beaumond Bread
Dawn Marshall

1 loaf of French bread
2 T. onion, minced
1/2 t. beaumond seasoning
8 to 12 oz. swiss cheese

1/2 lb. butter or margarine
1 t. dry mustard
2 t. lemon juice

Cut x's diagonally through the bread and then diagonally the other way, so the pieces of bread look like diamonds. DON'T cut all the way through. Mix butter, onion, mustard, lemon juice and seasoning. Slice cheese, put between the x's in the bread. You may have to use toothpicks to hold the shape of the bread. Cover the bread with the butter and spice mixture. Bake at 350 degrees for 30 minutes. Serve hot in one piece. Have everyone pull the bread apart.

Pumpkin Bread
Janie Milum

1 pkg. golden pound cake mix
1/3 c. water
1 c. canned pumpkin

2 eggs
1 t. baking soda
1 t. pumpkin pie spice

Heat oven to 325 degrees. Grease and flour 9" x 5" x 3" loaf pan. Blend all ingredients in a large mixer bowl. Beat for 3 minutes on medium speed. Pour batter into pan. Bake for 1 hour and 15 minutes, or until pick comes out clean. Cool for 10 minutes; remove from pan. If desired, serve with lemon butter.

Lemon Butter:

1/4 c. butter
juice and rind of 4 lemons

2 1/2 c. sugar
6 eggs, well beaten

In the top of a double-boiler, mix butter, sugar, eggs and lemon juice and rind. Be careful not to grate white part of the lemon peel into the mixture. Cook over boiling water, stirring, until thick. Pour into containers or glass jars. Cover and refrigerate.

Southern Biscuit Muffins

Kathy Bolyea

2 1/2 c. flour
1 1/2 T. baking powder
1 c. cold milk

1/4 c. sugar
3/4 c. cold margarine

Combine flour, sugar and baking powder. Cut in margarine until mixture resembles coarse crumbs. Stir in milk until flour mixture is moist. Spoon into muffin pan. Bake at 400 degrees for 20 minutes. Makes 12.

Cinnamon Nut Loaf

Julie Allen

1/4 c. brown sugar
1/4 c. chopped nuts
2 T. butter, softened
1 t. cinnamon
1/2 c. shortening
3/4 c. sugar
non-stick vegetable spray
2/3 c. undiluted evaporated milk

2 eggs
2 c. flour
1 t. baking powder
1 t. baking soda
1/2 t. salt
1/3 c. water
1 t. vanilla
1 T. vinegar

Combine brown sugar, nuts, butter and cinnamon; set aside. Spray 9" x 5" x 3" loaf pan with vegetable spray. Cream shortening, sugar and vanilla thoroughly. Add eggs, one at a time; beat well after each addition. Sift flour, baking powder, soda and salt together. Combine evaporated milk and water; stir in vinegar. Add flour mixture alternately with evaporated milk mixture to creamed mixture; blend well after each addition. Turn half the batter into prepared pan. Top with brown sugar-nut mixture. Spread with remaining batter. Bake in slow oven 325 degrees for 45 to 50 minutes or until inserted toothpick comes out clean. Makes 1 loaf.

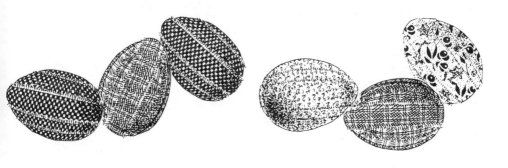

The Christmas Groaning Board

Cherry Blossom Muffins
Dorothy Moncrief

1 egg
2/3 c. orange juice
2 T. sugar
2 T. oil

2 c. biscuit baking mix
1/2 c. chopped pecans
1/2 c. cherry preserves
spicy topping

Combine egg, orange juice, sugar and oil. Add biscuit mix; beat vigorously for 30 seconds. Stir in nuts. Spray muffin pans with non-stick vegetable spray. Fill pans 1/3 full with batter. Top each with 2 teaspoons cherry preserves. Cover with remaining batter. Sprinkle with spicy topping. Bake at 400 degrees for 20 to 25 minutes. Makes 12 muffins.

Spicy Topping:
1/4 c. sugar
1/2 t. ground nutmeg

2 T. flour
1 T. butter

In a small bowl, mix thoroughly the sugar, nutmeg and flour. Cut in the butter until mixture is crumbly.

Orange Bran Loaf
Sharon Perry

3/4 c. orange juice
1 egg, slightly beaten
1/2 t. salt
1/4 t. baking soda
1 c. whole bran cereal

1/4 c. salad oil
1/2 c. sugar
1 c. flour
1 1/2 t. baking powder

Mix orange juice with bran. Add egg and oil, beating well. Sift flour, baking powder, soda, salt and sugar. Add the orange mixture, stirring only until combined. Pour into greased loaf pan. Bake at 350 degrees for 60 to 70 minutes or until done. Cool before slicing.

For an old-fashioned country Christmas, drape a quilt around the base of your tree instead of a tree skirt. If you have a live tree, be careful when watering and try not to spill!

Granma Lesieur's Mouth Watering "Banana Nut Bread"

Annie Wolfe
Gooseberry Patch

1 c. brown sugar
2 eggs
2 very ripe bananas, mashed
1/2 c. nuts (walnuts are the best)

1/2 c. shortening
2 c. flour, sifted
1 t. baking soda
1/2 t. salt

Cream shortening and add sugar. Cream well. Add eggs one at a time. Add mashed bananas and nuts. Sift dry ingredients together and add to shortening mixture. Pour batter into a greased bread pan. Bake at 350 degrees for 1 hour. Serve warm with butter or honey.

Annie's Famous Pumpkin Bread

Annie Wolfe
Gooseberry Patch

1/3 c. soft shortening
2 eggs
1/2 can (1 lb. can or 1 c.) pumpkin
1 1/2 c. plus 3 T. flour
1/4 t. baking powder
1/2 t. cloves, ground

1 1/3 c. sugar
1/3 c. water
1 t. baking soda
3/4 t. salt
1/2 t. cinnamon
1/3 c. walnuts, chopped

Mix shortening and sugar. Add eggs, pumpkin and water. Measure flour by dip method. Blend in flour, soda, salt, baking powder, cinnamon and cloves. Stir in nuts. Pour into a well greased pan. Bake at 350 degrees for 50 to 65 minutes.

The Christmas Groaning Board

Christmas Morning Cinnamon Rolls

Kimberly Burns

2 pkg. dry yeast
1/2 c. warm water (105-115 degrees)
1/3 c. plus 1/2 t. sugar
1 c. milk, scalded and cooled to 110 degrees

1 t. salt
1/3 c. oil
4 to 5 c. flour
2 eggs, room temperature

Filling:

1/2 c. soft butter
1 c. brown sugar

1/2 c. sugar
2 T. cinnamon

Icing:

1 t. vanilla
1 c. confectioners sugar, sifted

2 to 3 T. warm milk

In a cup, dissolve yeast in water with 1/2 teaspoon of sugar. Let stand for 5 minutes. In mixer bowl, combine 3 cups flour, remaining sugar and the salt. At low speed, gradually beat in milk, oil, eggs, and yeast mixture; beat until well blended. Beat in additional flour (about 1 1/2 cups) until dough pulls away from sides of bowl. On floured surface, knead dough until smooth and elastic, 8 to 10 minutes. Place in a greased bowl, turning to grease top. Cover and let rise in a warm, draft-free place until doubled in bulk, about 1 hour. In mixer bowl, beat all ingredients for filling until smooth. Set aside. Grease 2-9" round cake pans or 1- 9" x 13" cake pan. On a lightly floured surface, roll dough into an 18" x 10" rectangle. Spread with filling. Roll tightly from long side. Cut into 14- 1 1/4" slices, using a heavy piece of thread. Arrange rolls in pan. Cover and let rise until doubled in bulk, 30 to 40 minutes. Preheat oven to 350 degrees and bake for 25 to 30 minutes, until golden brown. Cool in pan for 10 minutes. Invert onto wire racks, then invert again to cool. Mix ingredients for icing until smooth. Drizzle over cooled rolls. Wrap well and freeze up to 1 month. Thaw, wrapped, at room temperature.

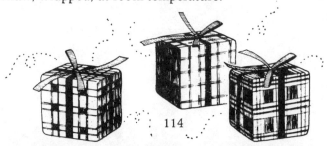

Lemon Fruitcake or Bread
Betty Richmond

1 lb. butter, softened
2 c. flour, sifted
2 oz. (bottle) lemon extract
2 c. walnuts or pecans, chopped

2 c. sugar
6 eggs, separated
1 c. white raisins

Cream butter, sugar and lemon extract. Beat egg yolks and add with raisins and nuts to the creamed mixture. Add flour, mixing well. Fold in well beaten egg whites. Pour into waxed paper lined pans. Bake at 250 degrees for 1 1/2 to 2 hours.

Apple Bread
Leigh Vaughn

1 1/2 c. oil
3 c. flour
1 1/2 c. sugar
3 eggs
1 can apple pie filling

1 t. salt
1 t. cinnamon
1 t. baking soda
1 t. vanilla

Mix all the ingredients together. Pour into two floured loaf pans and bake at 350 degrees for 1 hour. You may want to cover the tops with aluminum foil so they don't get too brown. Makes 2 loaves.

Easy Quiche Lorraine

9" pie shell, uncooked
6 slices of bacon
10 thin slices Swiss cheese
4 eggs, lightly beaten
1 c. heavy cream
1 c. whole milk

1 T. flour
ground nutmeg
cayenne pepper
2 T. diced onion
black pepper

Bake pie shell at 400 degrees for 10 minutes. Fry bacon until crisp and drain. Saute onion. Overlap bacon and cheese to cover bottom of the crust. Add onion. In a separate bowl combine eggs, cream, milk, flour with a pinch of nutmeg, cayenne and black pepper. Pour egg mixture over bacon and cheese. Bake at 400 degrees for 15 minutes then turn the oven down to 325 degrees for the last 30 minutes. Delicious with a cup of soup or fresh salad!

THe ChRISTmas GRoaNIng BoaRd

Poppyseed Bread

Susan Kirschenheiter

2 eggs
1 t. vanilla
1 1/2 c. sugar
1 t. baking powder
1/4 c. poppy seeds

1/2 c. oil
2 c. flour
1 t. salt
1 c. evaporated milk

Mix all ingredients together with mixer. Pour into 2 medium greased and floured loaf pans. Bake at 350 degrees for 1 hour. Test with toothpick for doneness. Makes 2 loaves.

Wonderful Pecan Rolls

12 muffin pan
36 pecan halves

1/2 c. brown sugar
1 stick (1/2 c.) butter

In muffin pan, put in each individual section, 2 teaspoons brown sugar, 2 teaspoons butter and 3 pecan halves.

2 c. biscuit baking mix
2/3 c. mashed bananas
15 caramels, melted
2 1/2 T. canned milk

1 t. cinnamon
2 T. butter, melted
1/4 c. brown sugar

Mix the biscuit baking mix, bananas and cinnamon and knead. Roll into a rectangle. Spread with butter. Spread caramels evenly across top. Sprinkle with brown sugar. Roll tightly. Slice into 12 pieces and put into individual muffin tins (right on top of the butter, brown sugar and pecans). Bake at 375 degrees for 8 to 10 minutes. Invert pan onto a cookie sheet or foil. Leave pan inverted for 1 to 2 minutes to let the butter and pecan mixture set into the pecan roll. Serve immediately.

To melt caramels: In double-boiler, combine canned milk and the caramels; melt slowly.

HEARTY COUNTRY FARE

The Christmas Groaning Board

The Juiciest-Ever Roast Turkey

Cotton Country Collection
Submitted by Karyl Bannister

1 turkey

Marinade:
1/4 c. dry mustard (4 T.)
2 T. worcestershire sauce
1/4 - 1/2 t. cider vinegar

2 1/2 T. olive oil
1 t. salt
1/8 t. freshly ground pepper

I'm giving you the quantities for the 9 1/2 lb. turkey I roasted. Make more of the marinade for a bigger one. Make this into a soft paste (more like a thick marinade) and paint it all over a well-thawed turkey, inside and out, a few hours before you're going to cook it, or the day before. I did it the day before, using my trusty 1 inch sash brush.

1 onion
1-2 stalks celery, cut to fit
some parsley

2 pieces of bacon
1 stick of butter

Inside, instead of stuffing, place onion, celery, parsley. Across the breast lay bacon and in the crevice between the drumstick and the body, tuck in chunks of butter. Soak a dish towel or piece of cheesecloth in olive oil and lay it over the turkey, which you put in an uncovered roaster. Add 1 to 2 cups stock from cooking the gizzard, neck, etc. (I used 1 1/2 cups; you could use chicken broth), for basting (right through the cheesecloth the whole time) only once or twice during the roasting. (I basted it lots more than that, but recipe says once or twice). Cook at 300, not 325, as is the usual turkey temp, according to this scale:

7-10 lb.	30 min. per lb.
10-15 lb.	20 min. per lb.
15-18 lb.	18 min. per lb.
18-20 lb.	15 min. per lb.
20-23 lb.	13 min. per lb.

I cooked my turkey a whole hour more than the scale shows, and it sure did not dry out the turkey, which gets the prize for juiciest ever. For gravy, the pan juices are abundant and richly flavorful, to thicken as you like. This turkey's a winner!

Egg and Sausage
Alfreda Crosley

2 c. stale bread, finely crumbled
1 c. sharp cheddar cheese, grated
1/2 c. or more chopped onion
1 c. mushrooms (optional)
1 t. dry mustard

1 lb. bulk pork sausage
6 eggs, slightly beaten
2 c. milk
1 t. salt

Fry, brown and drain sausage. Then crumble. In large bowl, beat eggs with a whisk. Add milk, salt, dry mustard, bread crumbs, cheese, onion and sausage, mixing well. Add mushrooms and mix. Pour into buttered 7" x 11" pan and refrigerate overnight. Bake at 350 degrees for 40 to 45 minutes until bubbly and lightly browned. Serves 6, but may be doubled to 12. When doubling use a 9" x 13" pan and bake for 1 hour.

Chicken Casserole Supreme
Gwen Linton

3 whole chicken breasts
1 can cream of mushroom soup
1/4 lb. butter, melted
8 oz. pkg. herb-seasoned stuffing mix

16 oz. sour cream
1 c. chicken broth

Stew chicken breasts, adding celery, onion, salt and pepper if desired, until meat falls off bones. Cube meat and mix with sour cream and soup. Put mixture in a 2-qt. casserole dish. Mix together stuffing mix, butter and broth, put on top of chicken. Bake at 350 degrees for 45 minutes. This is one of those amazing casseroles that is well liked by men, women, children and occasionally the family pet. Serve with cranberry sauce and a salad for lunch, add a vegetable for dinner.

To make "instant" wishes, put the wishbone from your holiday turkey in the microwave for 2-3 minutes rather than waiting days for it to dry!

Virginia Country Ham
Donna Fawcett

1 Virginia country ham
apple cider

Soak ham for 36 hours in cold water, changing water frequently. Place ham in a roasting pan and fill with apple cider. Cover and bake at 325 degrees for 20 minutes per pound. Slice thinly and serve.

Christmas Egg Casserole
Carol Davis

3/4 lb. medium sharp
    cheddar cheese, shredded
1 t. salt
6 eggs

12 slices bread, cubed
2 1/2 c. milk
1/2 t. dry mustard

Layer bread and cheese in a 9" x 13" greased baking pan. Beat eggs and mix together well the milk, salt and mustard. Pour over the bread. Let sit in the refrigerator overnight. Drizzle melted oleo over the top. Bake at 325 degrees for 40 to 60 minutes. Topping (optional): Top with one can of mushroom soup, 1/2 cup of sour cream and heat.

Glazed Corned Beef

3 lb. corned beef
1 c. dark orange marmelade
4 T. brown sugar

4 T. dijon-style
* mustard*

Place corned beef in a large pot and cover with boiling water. Bring to a boil, lower heat, cover partially and simmer as slowly as possible for about 3 hours, or until tender. (You could also cook meat slowly for several hours or overnight in a crockpot.) Preheat oven to 350 degrees. Mix marmelade, mustard and sugar together in a small bowl. Place meat on baking dish and cover with marmelade mixture. Bake for 30 minutes or until crisp. Serve hot!

Lentil and Mushroom Loaf With Savory Potato Filling

Nancie Gensler

1 c. raw lentils
2 cloves garlic, minced
5 oz. (1/2 pkg.) frozen spinach, thawed
1 c. firmly packed stilton or gruyere cheese, grated

1 T. safflower oil
6 oz. white mushrooms
1 T. natural soy sauce
2 T. wheat germ
freshly ground pepper
dash nutmeg

Rinse and sort the lentils. Combine in a heavy saucepan with 4 cups of water. Bring to a boil, then lower the heat and simmer, covered, until the lentils are tender, about 45 minutes. Drain. Preheat the oven to 350 degrees. Heat the oil in a large skillet. Add the garlic and mushrooms and saute over medium heat, stirring, until the mushrooms are wilted. Stir in the spinach, lentils, soy sauce, and wheat germ. Grind in some pepper, to taste, and add the nutmeg. Cook, stirring, until the mixture is heated through, then stir in the cheese. Lightly oil a 9" x 5" x 3" loaf pan, preferably glass. Pour in about 2/3 of the lentil mixture. Press some of the mixture up the sides of the pan to create a shell about 1/2" thick. Transfer the remaining lentil mixture to a small bowl and reserve until needed.

Filling:

1 T. safflower oil
1/4 c. dry bread crumbs
1/2 t. dried thyme
freshly ground pepper, to taste
1 c. coarsely mashed potato (from about 1 medium cooked and peeled potato)

1 c. chopped onion
1/2 t. seasoned salt
1/2 t. dried basil
curly parsley for garnish

Rinse the skillet, and heat the oil. Add the onion and saute until golden brown. Add the remaining filling ingredients and saute, stirring occasionally, for 5 minutes. Transfer into the shell created by the lentil mixture, then cover the top with the reserved lentil mixture. Bake for 40 to 45 minutes, or until the top is crusty. Remove from the oven and let the loaf stand for 10 to 15 minutes. Slide a spatula of knife around the edges to loosen it. Cut slices and arrange them on an oblong dish. Garnish with parsley and serve.

Fool Proof Prime Rib

Nancy Tomsen

1 standing or rolled rib roast   **fresh ground pepper**

The roast must be room temperature. Rub with fresh ground pepper. Place in a roasting pan (rib side down, if bones are in) and roast uncovered, in a preheated 375 degree oven, for exactly 1 hour. Turn oven off, but do not remove roast from oven. DO NOT open oven door at any time during this roasting period or while roast is resting in the oven. This can be done early in the day. About an hour before serving, set oven again to 325 degrees and continue roasting as follows:

2 rib roast - 25 minutes
3 rib roast - 30 minutes
4 rib roast - 35 minutes

The beef will be medium-rare throughout. Serves 8.

VEGETABLE CHILI

1 medium eggplant, cut in small cubes
2 medium yellow onion, diced
4 cloves garlic, finely chopped
2 large cans plum tomatoes (35 oz. each)
2 t. freshly ground black pepper
1 t. salt
1/2 c. chopped fresh parsley
1 can dark red kidney beans, drained

1 T. coarse or kosher salt
3/4 c. olive oil
2 large bell peppers, diced
2 T. chili powder
1 T. ground cumin
1 T. dried oregano
1 T. dried basil
1 t. fennel seed
1 can chick peas, drained
2 T. fresh lemon juice
1/2 c. fresh dill (dried will also do)

In a large skillet, over medium heat, saute 1/2 cup of olive oil and eggplant. Saute until tender. Pour softened eggplant into crock pot or large soup pan. In same skillet, saute remaining oil, onion, green pepper and garlic until softened. Add to eggplant mixture in crock pot or dutch oven. Slowly stir in, over low heat, tomatoes (crushed with hands), chili powder, cumin, oregano, basil, black pepper, salt, fennel seed and chopped parsley. Cook uncovered for at least 30 minutes. Can cook up to several hours depending on how well you like to simmer the vegetables! Stir in beans, dill and lemon juice. Stir to taste and adjust seasoning according to taste. Serve with brown rice and shredded cheddar cheese for a warm and wonderful harvest meal!

Egg Noodles

Patsy Grimmett

2 c. flour, sifted	4 eggs
1/4 t. salt	

Mix ingredients together to form a firm, but slightly sticky dough. Use lots of flour to avoid sticking. Separate dough into 4 parts. On a well-floured surface, roll each part separately until 1/8" thick. (The best noodles are from dough that is hard to roll.) After you get to the desired thickness, flour dough well again, and cut into wide lengthwise strips. Lay strips on top of each other, and, using a very sharp knife, cut into noodles about 1/2" thick. After all the noodles are cut, separate them on a large surface and allow to dry. Use in your favorite noodle recipe. Makes about 4 to 5 cups of dried noodles. Recipe may be increased by adding 2 eggs per additional cup of flour.

Christmas Day Brunch

Mary Kelly

1 lb. bulk sausage, browned	7 eggs
1 generous cup Gruyere or Cheddar	2 c. milk
cheese, shredded	1 t. dry mustard
3 slices white bread with crust, cubed	

Line the bottom of a 9" x 13" buttered casserole dish with the cubed bread. Beat eggs with milk and mustard. Layer bread with sausage, cheese and egg mixture. Cover and refrigerate overnight. Bake at 350 degrees for 35 minutes.

Apple-N-Sauerkraut Sausage

Sharon Hall
Gooseberry Patch

1 lb. kielbasa	2 c. apples, chopped
(cut in 1" pieces)	1/2 c. water
27 oz. can sauerkraut, washed	1/2 t. caraway seed
and drained	1/2 c. brown sugar, packed

Combine all ingredients in a frying pan. Cover. Simmer for 40 minutes until everything is tender.

Lee's Trim-The-Tree Turkey Tetrazzini

Lee Charrier

Cream Sauce:

4 T. margarine	4 T. flour
1 c. evaporated milk	1 c. whole milk
2 c. turkey or chicken stock	1/3 c. dry sherry

Combine in a large frying pan the margarine and flour. Add evaporated milk to the mixture. Stir while gradually adding the stock and whole milk. Continue to stir as it thickens. Add sherry and stir.

1 lb. fine spaghetti (broken into 3" to 4" pieces)	4 c. cream sauce
4 c. cubed, cooked turkey	12 oz. mushroom stems
1 c. mild cheddar cheese, grated	1/2 c. bread crumbs
	4 T. melted margarine

Cook spaghetti as directed. Saute mushrooms in 1 teaspoon oil and 1 teaspoon margarine. Mix spaghetti, cream sauce, mushrooms and turkey and place in a buttered 4-qt. or two 2-qt casserole dish. Mix the cheese, bread crumbs and margarine together, and cover the top. Bake at 425 degrees for 30 to 35 minutes. Cover for the first 15 minutes of baking and then uncover and it should bubble. Make ahead and refrigerate, bring out 1 hour before cooking.

Seasonal Sideboard

Marjoram THYME

Tarragon SAGE

PARSLEY

Oregano

VINEGARS Country Garden

Italian Herb Herbal G

Country Garden VINEGAR

Herbal Bala B

HERBS

The Christmas Groaning Board

Broccoli Casserole

Paul Gaulke
Gooseberry Patch

1 regular and 1 large bag of frozen broccoli
2 boxes chicken flavored rice vermicelli mix
2 cans cream of chicken soup
16 oz. pasteurized process cheese spread

Separately prepare broccoli and rice vermicelli mix according to package directions. Place cooked broccoli in a 4-qt. crockpot. Add cream of chicken soup to broccoli and stir. Cut up cheese, add to mixture in crockpot and stir. Stir in rice vermicelli mix. Allow time in heated crockpot for cheese to melt, and serve. Makes approximately 32-4oz. servings.

Try half broccoli and half cauliflower for a different version of this casserole. Delicious!

Company Potatoes

Valerie Bryan

5 lbs. potatoes
2 c. sour cream

8 oz. cream cheese
1/4 lb. margarine or butter

Wash, peel and cook potatoes until soft. Turn in to an electric mixer and add sour cream, cream cheese and margarine. Mix until smooth. Spoon into a greased 2-qt. casserole dish. Bake at 375 degrees for 45 minutes, or until bubbly. The depth of the casserole dish may cause a variance in the baking time. Company potatoes can be made days ahead of time and refrigerated. Perfect for a family gathering!

Holiday Cranberry Mold
Gwen Linton

3 oz. pkg. wild strawberry gelatin
    or any red flavor
3/4 c. cold water
2 c. raw cranberries
3 T. sugar

1 c. boiling water
1/2 small orange, peeled
1 medium apple, diced

Dissolve gelatin in boiling water, add cold water. Chill until thickened. Cut orange in wedges and remove seeds. Run orange and cranberries through food grinder, or chop in blender. Mix in apple and sugar, fold into thickened gelatin. Pour into 3-cup mold or 8 individual molds. Chill until firm. Recipe may be doubled for 1 1/2-qt. mold.

Lemon-Lime Salad
Gwendolyn Blackshire

1 pkg. lemon gelatin
1 small can crushed pineapple
    (Do not drain)
1 c. lemon-lime carbonated drink
1 c. boiling water

1 pkg. dry whipped
    topping mix
1 small pkg. cream cheese
1 c. chopped pecans

Dissolve lemon gelatin in boiling water. In another bowl, mix cream cheese and dry whipped topping mix. Mix in crushed pineapple. Slowly mix in gelatin mixture. Once blended well, slowly mix in carbonated drink. Pour mixture into serving dish. Cover the top with chopped pecans. Refrigerate until set. No matter how many other yummy goodies are made, everyone always goes for this dish. Lemon-lime salad is great year round and the yellow color is something a bit different on the plates.

Sweet Potato Casserole

Betty Byrd

2 lb. sweet potatoes
    (5 medium or 3 large)
1 T. cornmeal
3/4 c. sugar (or more to taste)
1/4 t. salt
raisins

1 stick margarine or butter
2 eggs
1/2 c. milk
1/4 t. nutmeg
1/2 t. vanilla

Cook potatoes in jackets until tender. Peel, then whip together with the other ingredients with mixer. Spoon into a baking dish. Bake at 350 degrees for about 30 minutes. Makes 6 servings.

TO GET THE "STRINGS" FROM THE SWEET POTATOES: Before adding other ingredients, put peeled potatoes in mixing bowl. Beat; lift beaters and rinse under water. Do this about three times. A small amount of potato is lost, but not enough to matter. This method truly takes care of the strings.

Holiday Apple and Cranberry Casserole

Kathi Stein

1 c. sugar
2 c. raw fresh cranberries
3 c. diced apples, unpeeled
    (hard or tart varieties)

1 c. quick oats
1/2 c. brown sugar
1 c. chopped pecans

Put the apples, cranberries and sugar in the bottom of a 9" x 13" well buttered casserole dish. Mix the oats, brown sugar and pecans and pour over the top of fruits. Dot the entire top with butter. Bake at 325 degrees for 1 hour.

Baby Baked Beans
Cindy Footit

1 lb. baby lima beans
3/4 lb. dark brown sugar

3 medium onions
1 lb. bacon

Soak beans overnight. Simmer beans with 1/2 onion until beans are tender. DON'T OVER COOK. Drain. Layer: Beans, onions, brown sugar and bacon. Bake at 325 degrees for 3 hours. One can add a little dark molasses for a little extra flavor, according to taste.

Mustard Sauce
Dorothy Moncrief

1 can tomato soup
1 c. vinegar, distilled
1 carton cholesterol-free imitation
    egg product

1 c. mustard
1 stick butter

Combine soup, vinegar, mustard and butter in a double-boiler. Cook until thickened. Then add egg product.

Cranberry Relish
Linda Brody

1 can crushed pineapple with juice
1/2 lb. miniature marshmallows
2 c. fresh cranberries, ground

1 c. sugar
1 c. whipped cream

Put crushed pineapple with juice over marshmallows, let stand overnight. Mix sugar in cranberries and let stand overnight. In the morning add all ingredients together and fold in whipped cream.

The Christmas Groaning Board

Sonia's Cranberry Ring

Sonia Bracamonte

1 can crushed pineapple, drained
1 regular size pkg. lemon gelatin
1 envelope unflavored gelatin

1 c. ground cranberries
1 t. grated lemon
1 t. grated orange rinds

Save juice from pineapple, after draining, to which enough water is added to make 2 cups of liquid. Boil the liquid. Combine gelatins in a bowl and add boiling liquid, stirring until dissolved. Add cranberries and grated rinds. Pour into ring and chill until firm. Diced walnuts may be added, if desired.

Auntie D's Salad

Donna Fox

1 c. mayonnaise
2 T. strawberry juice
1 c. frozen strawberries, thawed
1 c. whipping cream

3 oz. cream cheese
24 marshmallows
1 c. crushed pineapple

Place marshmallows and juice in a pan, heating slowly until melted. Put in a bowl and beat until smooth and fluffy. Allow to chill. Mix cream cheese and mayonnaise together. Blend in strawberries, pineapple and marsh-mallow mixture. Fold in whipping cream. Pour into an 8" cake pan or bread pan and freeze. Remove from freezer 30 minutes before serving.

Zucchini Bake

Kathy McFarlane

4 c. zucchini, sliced
1 c. mayonnaise
1 small green pepper, chopped
1/4 c. Parmesan cheese

2 eggs
1 T. butter
1 small onion, chopped
2 T. bread crumbs

Beat eggs in large bowl, add all the above ingredients except the bread crumbs. Grease a 9" x 13" x 2" pan. Pour mix in pan. Dot with butter and sprinkle with the bread crumbs. Bake at 350 degrees for 30 minutes.

Poppy Seed Dressing
Barbara Heck

1 1/2 c. sugar
2 t. salt
2 t. dry mustard
2/3 c. wine vinegar

1 T. minced onion
2 c. oil
3 T. poppy seed

Mix sugar, salt and mustard; stir in vinegar and onion. Gradually add oil, beating continuously until smooth (about 10 minutes). Stir in poppy seed. Refrigerate for 4 hours before serving.

Ambrosia
Sethora West

2 large cans crushed pineapple
    (not drained)
1 bottle maraschino cherries

2 doz. navel oranges
1 c. flaked coconut
sugar, as needed

Peel oranges, making sure all of the white pulp is taken off. Cut in small slices crosswise. Layer oranges and pineapple in a trifle bowl. After each layer of oranges, sprinkle with sugar. End the layers with pineapple and then add a layer of coconut (be sure it covers the top). Cut up cherries on top of coconut. Let stand in refrigerator over night.

Onion and Apple Casserole
Betty Richmond

1 1/2 lb. tart apples
4 T. butter
3/4 t. cinnamon

1 large onion
2 T. brown sugar
3 T. soaked currants

Peel, core and slice apples thinly. Line bottom of a casserole dish with 1/3 of the apples. Coarsely chop the onion and saute in 3 tablespoons of butter, until translucent. Turn off heat and add brown sugar, currants and cinnamon. Put half of the mixture on top of the apples, then add 1/3 more apples, the rest of the onion mixture and the remainder of apples. Dot with butter. Bake at 350 degrees for 45 minutes. Serves 6 to 8.

My Favorite Salad Dressing

Aundra Zack

4 t. dry mustard
4 t. salt
1 1/3 c. wine vinegar
1 T. celery salt

2 c. sugar
1 medium onion, grated
1 qt. vegetable oil
1 t. garlic salt

Combine sugar, mustard, salt, onion and vinegar in blender and beat well. Add oil and beat until thick. Store in a glass container with a lid. This recipe makes alot, you can make 1/2 the recipe if you wish. Good when used on a tossed salad or fresh spinach. Do not add onion to your salad, it is already in the dressing.

Christmas Crunch Salad

Aundra Zack

2 bunches fresh broccoli
    (broken in small pieces)
1 head cauliflower
    (broken in small pieces)

1 red onion, chopped
2 c. cherry tomatoes
    (cut in half)

Dressing:
1 c. mayonnaise
1 T. vinegar
dash of salt and pepper
1/2 c. sour cream
2 T. sugar

Combine dressing ingredients, mix well. Toss with vegetables. Serve well chilled. Can be done a day ahead, and is particularly pretty if served in a clear glass bowl. Serves 6.

Candied Sweets
Lois Eisenhut

6 medium sweet potatoes,
   cooked and peeled
1/2 c. miniature marshmallows

3/4 c. brown sugar
1 t. salt
1/4 c. butter

Slice potatoes into 1/2" slices. Layer potatoes in a buttered 1 1/2-qt. casserole dish with mixture of sugar, salt and butter on top. Continue until ending with sugar and butter. Bake uncovered at 375 degrees for about 30 minutes or until glazed. Add marshmallows in the last 5 minutes; brown lightly. Serves 6.

Harvest Dressing
Debra Himes

1 c. carrots, shredded
1/2 c. onion, chopped
1/2 c. butter or margarine
1/4 t. cinnamon
3/4 c. chicken broth
8 c. whole wheat or white bread
   cubes (or 4 c. each)
2 c. peeled apples, finely chopped

1 c. celery, chopped
1 t. poultry seasoning
1/2 t. salt
1/8 t. pepper
1/4 c. wheat germ
1/2 c. walnuts, chopped

Cook carrots, celery and onion in butter until tender, but not brown. Stir in all the seasonings. Add the chicken broth. In a large bowl, combine all the other ingredients. Pour the liquid mixture over this and toss lightly. Put in lightly buttered bowl and cover, or put in your turkey. Bake at 350 degrees for 50 minutes. Makes 6 servings.

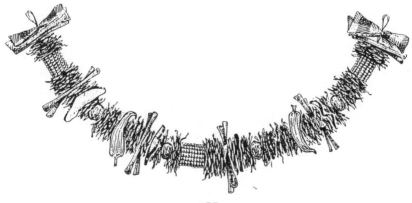

The ChrisTmas GroaNiNg Board

Grandma Liz's Turkey Dressing
Susan Kirschenheiter

1 1/2" diameter onion
giblets from turkey
1/4 c. raisins
12 slices wheat bread, dried out
  and cubed

2 stalks celery
2 eggs, beaten
2 t. salt
1 t. pepper

Grind up onion, celery and giblets in a grinder. Add bread, eggs, raisins, salt and pepper; mix well. Put mixture in cleaned turkey and cook as usual.

Frozen Cranberry Salad
Phyllis Frump

1 banana, mashed
1 small can crushed pineapple
  undrained

1 small container frozen
  whipped topping
1 small can cranberry
  sauce or relish

Combine all ingredients and then freeze. Take out freezer about 30 minutes before serving. This recipe doubles easily. You can also add pecans, if desired.

Sweet Potato Filled Pumpkin
Linda Crowley

3 c. cooked, mashed sweet potatoes
1/2 c. sugar
1/4 c. milk
1/3 c. butter, melted
2 eggs, beaten
1 t. vanilla
2-qt. size pumpkin, circular lid cut
  out and seeds & fiber removed

Topping:
1/3 c. all-purpose flour
1 c. chopped pecans
1 c. flaked coconut
1 c. brown sugar
1/3 c. butter, melted

Combine sweet potatoes, sugar, milk, butter, beaten eggs and vanilla. Fill the hollowed-out pumpkin with the mixture. Mix together flour, pecans, coconut, brown sugar, and melted butter. Sprinkle over top of potato mixture. Place the filled pumpkin in a greased baking dish. Top with "lid" (top of pumpkin) and bake for 45 minutes at 375 degrees. Remove lid and bake an additional 15 minutes, or until golden brown. Allow pumpkin to cool for 10 to 15 minutes before serving. Note: an ice cream scoop works very well for scraping out the pumpkin.

Cranberry Sauce
Linda Crowley

2 lb. whole berry cranberry sauce
6 T. orange liqueur

6 T. lemon juice
1 t. dry mustard

Mix all the ingredients. Boil until reduced one-fourth. This will make your holiday turkey unforgettable.

Enid's Spinach-Cheese Casserole
Karyl Bannister

2-10 oz. pkg. frozen chopped spinach
1 can cream of mushroom soup
2 eggs, beaten

1 c. mayonnaise
1 c. shredded cheddar cheese
1/4 c. chopped onion

Cook spinach and drain, squeezing out all moisture. Combine with rest of ingredients and turn into large, buttered casserole. Enid and I like one big enough so the spinach isn't much deeper than about 2 1/2". Bake 45 minutes at 350 degrees. Serves 12

Red and Green Slaw
Karyl Bannister

1 1/2 c. chopped green cabbage
    (chopped or very thinly sliced
    is much nicer than shredded)
1/2 c. red cabbage, ditto

1/2 of a sweet red pepper,
    sliced ever so thinly
    in long strips

Dressing:
1/4 c. mayonnaise
1 t. lime juice
pinch sugar

1/4 t. garlic
salt

Combine and serve. Yes, red sweet peppers are costly. But they are so good, and you deserve one, this time. Serves 8 to 10

The Christmas Groaning Board

Hot Sausage Dressing (on the side)

Betsy Allport
submitted by Karyl Bannister

1 lb. hot good sausage
7-10 stalks celery, chopped fine
3 large onions, chopped fine
1/2-3/4 c. snipped fresh parsley
1 lb. pkg. herb-seasoned stuffing
  mix, not cubes
2 eggs
salt and pepper

1 stick butter/margarine
lots of snipped fresh sage &
  thyme, if available, or
1-2 T. dried sage and
1-2 t. dried thyme
few shakes of poultry
  seasoning
milk

Saute sausage, breaking it up in small bits. Drain off fat and set aside. In large bowl mix celery, onion, parsley, and stuffing mix. Beat eggs and add with fresh or dried herbs and seasonings. Add milk, blending a small amount at a time, until mixture is of dressing consistency. Fold in cooked sausage. Taste and correct seasonings. Put in containers to freeze or in pottery dishes to bake as soon as the turkey-bird comes out of the oven to await carving. Bake 20 minutes at 350 degrees (size of container determines time; don't let it dry out). Serves 8

EASY CHEESY SCALLOPED POTATOES

8 c. thinly sliced potatoes
3 c. flour
3 c. milk or cream
6 T. butter
1/2 red pepper, chopped
1/2 green pepper, chopped

8 oz. colby cheese, shredded
1 med. onion, chopped
6 slices bacon, fried crisp
2 1/2 t. salt
1/2 t. mustard
1/2 t. paprika

Grease a large casserole baking dish. Shake thinly sliced potatoes in a bag with flour and place in casserole in 4 layers: potatoes, cheese, onions, peppers, crumbled bacon and dot with butter. Heat milk, salt, paprika and mustard until hot and pour mixture evenly over the potatoes. Bake at 350 degrees for 1 1/2 hours, covering for the first half hour. Serves 10.

YULETIDE Sweets

No-Cook Mints
Joan Schaeffer

1/3 c. light Karo syrup
1 t. peppermint extract
4 3/4 c. sifted powdered sugar

1/4 c. butter, softened
1/2 t. salt
red and green food coloring

Blend Karo syrup, butter, peppermint extract, salt and powdered sugar; mix with spoon and hands til smooth. Divide into thirds; knead 1 drop of red food coloring into one third and 1 drop of green food coloring into another third. Leave remaining third white. Shape into small balls; flatten with fork on waxed paper lined baking sheets. Let dry several hours. Yields 72 patties.

Peach-A-Berry Cobbler
Cheryl Todd

1 T. cornstarch
1/4 c. brown sugar
1/2 c. cold water
2 c. sugared fresh peaches

1 c. fresh blueberries
1 T. butter
1 T. lemon juice

Mix cornstarch, sugar and water, add peaches and blueberries. Cook and stir until mixture thickens. Add butter and lemon juice. Pour into an 8" x 8" baking dish. (Use frozen fruit or use canned, draining the juice and using it in place of water.)

Cobbler Crust:
1 c. flour, sifted
1/2 c. sugar
1 1/2 t. baking powder

1/2 t. salt
1/2 c. milk
1/4 c. butter, softened

Sift dry ingredients together. Add milk and butter all at once. Heat until smooth. Spread over cobbler mixture. Mix 2 tablespoons sugar with 1/4 tablespoon nutmeg and sprinkle over cobbler. Bake at 350 degrees for 30 minutes. Serve warm with cream. Makes 6 to 8 servings.

Pumpkin Cake Roll

Lisa Murch

3 eggs
2/3 c. pumpkin
3/4 c. flour
2 to 3 t. pumpkin pie spice
1 c. finely chopped walnuts or pecans

1 c. sugar
1 t. lemon juice
1 t. baking powder
1/2 t. salt

Beat eggs on high speed for 5 minutes. Gradually beat in sugar. Stir in pumpkin and lemon juice. Next stir together flour, baking powder, salt and pumpkin pie spice. Fold into pumpkin mixture. Spread in greased and floured 15" x 10" x 1" pan. Top with nuts. Bake at 375 degrees for 15 minutes. Turn out on towel sprinkled with powdered sugar. Starting at narrow end, roll towel and cake together and let cool. Unroll.

Filling:

1 c. powdered sugar
6 oz. cream cheese

4 T. butter
1/2 t. vanilla

Combine powdered sugar, cream cheese, butter and vanilla. Beat until smooth. Spread over cake and roll. Chill.

Optional Nutmeg Sauce:

1 c. sugar
2 T. all-purpose flour
1/2 t. nutmeg

2 c. water
1 T. butter
1 T. white or cider vinegar

Combine sugar, flour and nutmeg in 2-qt. saucepan. Add water and stir while heating to a boil. Reduce heat and boil gently for 5 minutes. Stir frequently. Remove from heat and stir in butter and vinegar. Serve hot over pumpkin cake roll.

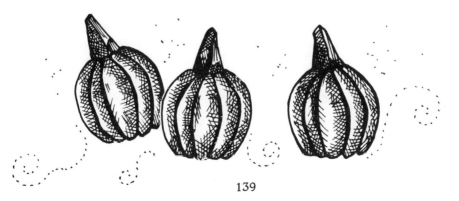

The Christmas Groaning Board

Scripture Cake
Cheryl Todd

A favorite baking "conceit" for ladies in the 20th century, Scripture Cake required that the cook use the Bible to discover what ingredients were needed in the recipe. And since some of the Biblical passages were vague about the exact sweetenings, spices, fruits and nuts that were to be used, several varieties of Scripture Cakes can be found in the older cookbooks. This one is a spice cake; others resemble fruitcakes.

1/2 c. Judges 5:25, last clause
Jeremiah 6:20
2 T. I Samuel 14:25
6 Jeremiah 17:11
1 1/2 c. I Kings 4:22
2 t. Amos 4:5

II Chronicles 9:9, to taste
Pinch of Leviticus 2:13
1/2 c. Judges 4:19, last clause
2 c. Nahum 3:12
2 c. Numbers 17:8
2 c. I Samuel 30:12

Whip the Judges, Jeremiah and I Samuel until light. Beat the 6 Jeremiah yolks and add to mixture. Add Kings, Amos, Chronicles and Leviticus, alternately with Judges. Fold in Nahum, Numbers and Samuel, then also the Jeremiah whites, beaten stiff. Bake 2 hours in a greased 10" tube pan at 300 degrees.

Interpretation of Scripture Cake

1/2 c. butter
2 c. sugar
2 T. honey
6 egg yolks
1 1/2 c. flour, sifted
2 t. baking powder
2 t. cinnamon
1/2 t. ginger

1 t. nutmeg
1/2 t. cloves
pinch of salt
1/2 c. milk
2 c. figs, chopped
2 c. raisins
2 c. almonds
6 egg whites, beaten stiff

Beat together the butter, sugar, and honey. Beat the egg yolks and add sifted flour, baking powder, spices and salt, alternately with the milk. Stir in the figs, raisins and almonds. Fold in the 6 egg whites which have been beaten stiff. Bake the cake in a well greased 10" tube pan. Lining the pan with greased brown paper may provide added protection. Bake at 300 degrees for 2 hours.

Holiday Fruitcake

Kathy-Leigh Russo

There have been lots of jokes about inedible and tasteless fruitcakes that nobody in their right mind would eat, but this fruitcake is always greeted with cheers and devoured.

2 1/2 c. flour, sifted
1 t. baking soda
2 eggs, slightly beaten
1 jar (28 oz.) mincemeat
1 can (15 oz.) sweetened
    condensed milk
1/4 c. apricot brandy (optional)

1 lb. mixed candied fruit
1/2 lb. red candied cherries
1 1/2 c. walnuts, coarsely
    chopped

Preheat the oven to 300 degrees. Butter the baking pans, then line with waxed paper and spray the waxed paper with non-stick spray. Sift together the flour and baking soda; set aside. Combine the eggs, mincemeat and sweetened condensed milk. Stir in the fruit and nuts. Stir in the flour mixture. Turn into the pans. Decorate the tops of the cakes with walnut halves and red and green candied cherries, if desired. Bake until the center springs back when touched and the top is golden. Cool. Turn out and remove waxed paper. When completely cool, wrap first in new waxed paper, then in foil. Store in a cool place for up to 6 weeks.

1 recipe yields 1-9" tube or springform pan OR 3 or 4 loaf pans.
1-9" tube or springform pan = 2 hours baking time.
3 or 4 loaf pans = 1 hour, 25 minutes baking time.

Walnut Crescents

Heidi Hosler

1 c. margarine, softened
2 t. vanilla
1/4 t. salt

1 c. chopped nuts
1 3/4 c. flour
1/2 c. confectioners sugar

Cream margarine. Add sugar, vanilla and salt. Beat until light. Stir in nuts and flour until well blended. Wrap dough in waxed paper and chill in refrigerator overnight. Preheat oven to 300 degrees. Divide dough into 8 parts. While working with one part keep the others refrigerated. Shape one section into a long roll. Cut roll into 2" pieces. Shape each piece into a crescent shape. Put crescents on an ungreased cookie sheet. Bake for 18 to 20 minutes. Cool on a rack. Sift confectioners sugar over tops. Repeat with other 7 sections. Store in an airtight container.

Old-Fashioned Filled Cookies
Linda Meyers

1/2 c. butter or margarine
1 c. sugar
2 eggs
2 T. milk
2 1/2 c. flour
1/4 t. baking soda
1/2 t. salt

1/2 c. raisins
1/2 c. dates
1/2 c. figs
1/2 c. sugar
1/2 c. water
2 t. lemon juice
2 t. vanilla

Cream butter and sugar until fluffy. Add eggs; beat well. Sift together dry ingredients and add to creamed mixture alternately with milk, beating well after each addition. Cover and chill dough at least 3 hours. In food processor or grinder chop raisins, dates and figs until fine. Combine remaining ingredients in saucepan and mix well. Cook over medium heat, stirring constantly, until it comes to a boil. Simmer for 2 minutes. Remove from heat and cool completely.

Divide dough into fourths. Use one fourth at a time, keeping remaining dough in refrigerator. Roll out each fourth of the dough on floured surface to 1/8" thickness. With floured 2 1/2" round cookie cutter, cut 18 rounds from each fourth. Place rounds about 2" apart on greased baking sheets. Place about 1 teaspoon of filling in center of each round. Spread filling with back of spoon to flatten. Top each with another round. Crimp edges with a fork, if desired. Bake at 375 degrees for 10 to 12 minutes or until golden brown. Let cool on racks. Makes 3 dozen.

Chocolate-Covered Peanut Butter Cracker Cookies
Margaret O'Hara

Christmas sprinkles
chocolate and white chocolate melting
    disks (from baking supply store)

round buttery-flavored
    crackers
peanut butter

Spread 2 crackers with peanut butter and put together. Dip in melted chocolate and place on waxed paper. While chocolate is still wet, decorate with sprinkles and candies.

The Christmas Groaning Board

Snowman Treat
Diane Waldron

1 batch krispy rice treats
mini chocolate chips

red and green candy coated
milk chocolate candies
red shoelace licorice

Make 1 batch of krispy rice treats and while still warm form into 3" balls. Stack 2 balls together. Use the candy coated milk chocolate candies for buttons, mini chocolate chips for eyes and the licorice for a scarf.

Nell Eales' Butter Cookies
Donna Fawcett

My good neighbor Eleanor (Nell) Eales, who was childless adopted the neighborhood children as her own. She played Easter Bunny, hiding candies and gifts in special places in the yards, or leaving them at the door, to be discovered on Easter Sunday by the children. Each Christmas she would bake delicious sugar cookies for all her neighbors. Nell has Alzheimer's disease and has been in a coma state for the past seven years. We all miss this wonderful person and would like to have a small memorial – her cookie recipe in your book.

1 c. butter
2 1/2 c. flour
1 T. lemon extract

1 c. sugar
1 T. vanilla extract
1 large egg

Cream butter and sugar. Add beaten egg, flour and extracts, mix well. Make tiny balls and dip in colored sugar. Flatten balls and put on baking sheets. Bake at 350 degrees for 12-14 minutes.

Snow Ice Cream

2 eggs
1/2 c. condensed milk

4 T. sugar
1 T. vanilla

Combine all ingredients and beat well. Collect pail of freshly fallen snow. Beat mixture into snow. For an extra special treat, drizzle blueberry, maple or strawberry syrup over top—yum!

Kentucky Whiskey Cake
Donna Fawcett

5 c. flour
1 c. brown sugar
6 eggs, separated
1 lb. pecans
1 lb. marachino cherries
    (red and green)

2 c. sugar
1 1/2 c. butter
1 pt. bourbon
1/2 lb. white raisins
1 t. baking powder

Soak cherries and raisins in bourbon overnight. Cream butter and sugar, add soaked fruit and remaining liquid. Add egg yolks, beaten. Dust pecans with a little flour, then fold the rest of the flour into the sugar mixture, along with the baking powder. Stiffly whip the egg whites and fold into mixture. Add the pecans. Pour into a tube pan and bake at 300 degrees for about 2 hours.

Chocolate Covered Cherries
Donna Fawcett

2-10 oz. jars marachino cherries
1 stick margarine, softened
1 T. evaporated milk
8 oz. semi-sweet chocolate

1 lb. confectioners sugar
2 t. vanilla
1/4 square paraffin

Mix together sugar, margarine, vanilla and milk. Wrap mixture around the cherries. Chill overnight. Melt chocolate and paraffin together, and dip cherries in the mixture.

Old-Fashioned Tea Cakes
Dianne Wells

1 c. sugar
1 egg
1 t. vanilla (or other flavoring)
1/2 t. salt

1 stick margarine
1 3/4 c. plain flour
1/4 t. baking soda

Knead and roll on floured cloth. Cut with a cookie cutter and place on a greased cookie sheet. Dough may also be dropped by teaspoonsful onto sheet and then pressed with the bottom of a glass that has been greased and dipped in sugar. Bake at 300 degrees for 10 to 15 minutes or until lightly browned. Add nuts, spice, raisins or coconut, if desired.

Chocolate Sheet Cake
Bonnie Jennings

2 c. sugar
1 t. baking soda
4 T. cocoa
3/4 c. buttermilk
1 t. vanilla

2 c. flour
2 sticks oleo
1 c. water
2 eggs

Sift together sugar, flour and baking soda. Next, melt oleo and cocoa in the water. Bring to a rapid boil. Pour over dry ingredients, stir until well mixed. Mix in the buttermilk, eggs and vanilla. Pour into an ungreased 12" x 18" x 1" pan. Bake at 350 degrees for 15 to 20 minutes.

Fudge Icing:
1 stick oleo
6 T. buttermilk
1 box confectioners sugar

4 T. cocoa
1 t. vanilla
1 c. nuts (if desired)

Melt oleo and cocoa in the buttermilk. Bring to a boil. Add confectioners sugar, vanilla and nuts. Spread on hot cake.

Buckeyes
Matt & Emily Hutchins
VICKIE'S KIDS

2 sticks margarine
1 1/2 lb. powdered sugar
1/2 square paraffin

1 lb. peanut butter
12 oz. pkg. chocolate chips

Easy to make and always a favorite, these resemble buckeyes or horse chestnuts (depending on what part of the country you're from) and are absolutely scrumptious! Mix the margarine, peanut butter and powdered sugar together. Form small balls. Chill. Melt chocolate and paraffin. Using toothpicks, dip peanut butter balls into chocolate leaving a small spot uncoated. Let cool on waxed paper.

THE HUTCHINS HOME EST. 1989

Christmas Hermit Cookies

Bonnie Jennings

2 c. sugar
3 eggs
1 c. raisins
1 t. cinnamon
1 t. nutmeg
1/2 t. baking powder

1 c. shortening
1/2 c. milk
1 c. nut meats
1 t. cloves
1 t. baking soda
6 c. flour

Combine all ingredients. Roll dough as thin as possible, but use your own judgment. Cut with glass with sugar on the rim. Bake at 325 to 350 degrees. Keep track of the time.

Chocolate Animal Crackers

Judy Norris

1 large box animal crackers
12 oz. semi-sweet chocolate bits

1 small piece of paraffin
2 T. vegetable shortening

Melt chocolate and shortening in pan. Add paraffin. Stir until smooth. Dip animal crackers into chocolate, covering both sides. Lift out with fork. Place on wax paper. While still hot, sprinkle with colored sugar sprinkles. Allow to harden. Store in airtight tin.

Cinnamon Sticks "1886"

Joyce Lolich

1 c. shortening
1/2 c. sugar

1 egg yolk
1 3/4 c. flour

Mix all ingredients. Roll and cut into finger lengths. Roll sticks in cinnamon and sugar. Bake at 350 degrees until set and edges are light brown.

The Christmas Groaning Board

Grandma Josephine's Oatmeal Cookies
Jane Bratton

When her daughter was a young bride, Josephine gave her this recipe. That young bride is now 76 and has passed it on to the next generation.

2 c. flour	1 t. baking soda
1 1/4 t. cinnamon	1 t. nutmeg
2 c. quick oats	1/2 c. brown sugar
1/2 c. sugar	1 c. vegetable shortening
2 eggs, unbeaten	1/3 c. milk
1 c. raisins and chopped walnuts	1 t. vanilla

In a large bowl, sift together flour, baking soda, cinnamon and nutmeg. Add all the other ingredients except raisins and walnuts. Beat for 2 minutes, using a mixer. You will have to stop and scrape the beaters occasionally. Add the raisins and walnuts. Bake at 375 degrees for 10 minutes.

Santa's Whiskers
Joyce Lolich

2 1/2 c. all-purpose flour	1 c. butter or margarine
1/2 c. pecans, finely chopped	1 c. sugar
3/4 c. flaked coconut	2 T. milk
3/4 c. finely chopped red or green candied cherries	1 t. vanilla or rum flavor

In mixing bowl cream butter or margarine, and sugar together. Blend in milk and vanilla. Stir in flour, chopped candies and pecans. Form dough into two 8" rolls. Roll in flaked coconut to coat outside. Wrap in waxed paper and chill thoroughly. Cut into 1/4" slices. Place on an ungreased cookie sheet. Bake at 375 degrees for about 12 minutes or until edges are golden. Makes about 60.

Christmas Fruitcake
Juanita Rieser

1 lb. butter
1 lb. flour
1 lb. sugar
10 eggs, beaten
2 lb. raisins (white and dark)
1 lb glazed cherries
2 lb. glazed pineapple
1/8 c. white port wine

2 t. cinnamon
2 t. mace
2 t. cloves
1 t. nutmeg
1/2 c. molasses
2 t. lemon extract
2 t. orange extract
1 c. nuts

Glaze:
1/4 c. light corn syrup

2 T. white port wine

Combine and bring to a rolling boil. Remove from heat and cool to luke-warm. Brush on cooled fruitcakes.

Cream butter. Gradually add sugar and continue creaming. Add beaten eggs and mix well. Add extract, wine and molasses. Sift dry ingredients together add to mixture. Stir in mixed fruits. Use 3 loaf pans that have been greased and lined with waxed paper. Fill loaf pans about 2/3 full. Bake at 325 degrees for 1 1/2 hours or more or until pick comes out clean. Cool and then glaze. Store in airtight tin box or wrap in foil. Makes 3 large loaves.

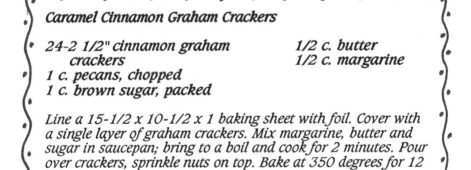

Caramel Cinnamon Graham Crackers

24-2 1/2" cinnamon graham
    crackers
1 c. pecans, chopped
1 c. brown sugar, packed

1/2 c. butter
1/2 c. margarine

Line a 15-1/2 x 10-1/2 x 1 baking sheet with foil. Cover with a single layer of graham crackers. Mix margarine, butter and sugar in saucepan; bring to a boil and cook for 2 minutes. Pour over crackers, sprinkle nuts on top. Bake at 350 degrees for 12 minutes. Cut into triangles. Yields 4 dozen.

Big Soft Ginger Cookies

Rebecca Ilgen

2 1/4 c. flour
1 t. baking soda
1/2 t. ground cloves
1/4 t. salt (optional)
1 egg
2 T. sugar

2 t. ground ginger
3/4 t. ground cinnamon
3/4 c. margarine
1 c. sugar
1/4 c. molasses

Combine flour, ginger, baking soda, cloves and salt and set aside. Place margarine in a large bowl. Beat with mixer on low speed for 30 seconds to soften. Gradually add the cup of sugar. Beat until fluffy. Add egg and molasses, beating well. Stir dry ingredients into beaten mixture. Shape into 1 1/2" balls (about 1 heaping teaspoon of dough). Roll in the 2 tablespoons of sugar, and place on an ungreased cookie sheet about 2 1/2" apart. Bake at 350 degrees for about 10 minutes, or until light brown and still puffed. DO NOT OVERCOOK. Let stand 2 minutes then put on wire rack to cool. Makes 24-3" cookies.

Cowboy Cookies

Ryan & Kyle Martin
JOANN'S KIDS

Our favorite cookies, here's the recipe for those little cowboys and indians in your house!

3 c. shortening
3 c. brown sugar
2 t. vanilla
1/2 t. salt
2 large pkg. chocolate chips
1/2 T. baking powder

6 eggs
3 c. white sugar
6 c. flour
6 c. rolled oats
1 T. baking soda

Cream together shortening, eggs, sugars and vanilla. Sift flour, salt, baking soda and baking powder. Slowly stir dry mixture into creamed mixture. Add rolled oats and chocolate chips; mix evenly. Bake at 350 degrees for 12 to 15 minutes. Makes several dozen depending on the size of the cookies you like.

JOANN'S ♥ COUNTRY ♥ KITCHEN

Whoopie Pies

Rebecca Ilgen

1 c. sugar
1 egg
1 egg yolk (save white for filling)
2/3 c. unsweetened cocoa powder
1/2 c. hot water

1/2 c. shortening
2 c. flour
1/4 t. salt
1 t. baking soda
2/3 c. buttermilk

In a mixer, on high speed, beat together sugar and shortening, until fluffy. Add the egg and egg yolk. In a separate bowl, stir together the flour, cocoa powder and salt; set aside. Dissolve the baking soda in hot water; cool slightly. Add the flour mixture, the soda mixture, and the buttermilk mixture alternately to the creamed mixture. Beat until well mixed. Drop batter by rounded teaspoonful 2" apart on an ungreased cookie sheet. Bake at 350 degrees for 8 to 10 minutes. Let cool on racks.

Filling:
2 c. powdered sugar, sifted
1 t. vanilla
1/4 c. butter or margarine, softened

1 egg white
1/2 c. shortening

Combine powdered sugar, egg white, and vanilla in mixing bowl, beating at low speed. Gradually add shortening and the butter or margarine. Beat at high speed until fluffy. Spread some filling on the flat side of half of the cookies; top with remaining cookies, flat side down. Store in refrigerator. Makes 24.

Chocolate Truffle Cookie
Rebecca Ilgen

4 oz. unsweetened chocolate
2 c. (12 oz.) semi-sweet chocolate
   chips
2 T. unsweetened cocoa powder
1 c. sugar
1 1/2 t. vanilla

6 T. butter
1/2 c. flour
1/4 t. baking powder
1/4 t. salt
3 eggs

Chop up unsweetened chocolate. Cut butter into pieces and melt in double boiler with 1 cup of chocolate chips, stirring occasionally. Cool. In separate bowl, mix together flour, cocoa, baking powder and salt. With mixer, beat the sugar and eggs about 2 minutes. Beat in vanilla. Stir in chocolate mixture, then flour mixture and finally the remaining 1 cup of chocolate chips. Cover and chill until firm, at least 1 hour. Heat oven to 350 degrees. Shape into approximately 1" balls. Place on an ungreased cookie sheet about 2" apart. Bake for about 10 minutes, until puffed. Makes 4 dozen.

Butter Cookies
Cindy Footit

1 lb. butter
2 c. sugar
8 c. flour

1 lb. margarine
1 egg

Mix ingredients together. Use a cookie press or make rolls and roll them in colored sugar. Chill and slice. Bake at 325 degrees until just set or barely golden brown.

Make a homemade pastry tube with a resealable plastic sandwich bag. Fill it halfway with the frosting, then close it up. Cut a tiny hole in one corner and you're ready to decorate!

Frosted Nutmeg Logs
Elane Crum

1 c. butter or margarine
1 1/4 t. nutmeg
2 t. rum extract
3 c. all-purpose flour

3/4 c. sugar
1 egg
2 t. vanilla extract

Cream butter and sugar. Add nutmeg, egg and extracts, mixing thoroughly. Sift flour and measure; stir into creamed mixture. Shape into rolls 1/2" in diameter and 3" long. Place about 2" apart on ungreased baking sheet. Bake at 350 degrees for 15 minutes or until lightly browned. Cool. Frost with Vanilla-Rum Frosting. Makes 3 to 4 dozen.

Vanilla-Rum Frosting:
1/4 c. butter, softened
1 t. vanilla
2 T. cream

3 c. powdered sugar
1 t. rum extract
nutmeg

Cream butter until soft and fluffy. Add part of the sugar and extracts, mixing well. Add remaining sugar and enough of the cream to obtain the desired spreading consistency. Frost cookies and run the tines of a fork down the frosting. Sprinkle with nutmeg. Makes 1 1/3 cups frosting.

Grandma Booth's Clifford Tea Christmas Cookies
Jeanne Elmer

1 c. butter (no substitute)
2 eggs
1 t. baking soda
1 c. chopped nuts

2 c. brown sugar
3 1/2 c. flour
1/2 t. salt

Cream together butter and sugar. Add eggs and beat. Sift flour, salt and nuts together. Add to butter mixture. Mix. Shape into rolls. Roll in waxed paper and chill overnight. Slice and bake at 325 degrees for 15 minutes or until golden brown.

> *Mix up your own potpourri with bay leaves, herbs, pepperberries, orange peel, cinnamon sticks, miniature pomanders scented with rich, delicious cinnamon oil!*

The Christmas Groaning Board

Fuddpuckers

Deborah Evans

1 pkg. peanut butter
   cookie dough
chopped pecans

40 small peanut butter filled
   chocolate candies

Cut package of cookie dough in half after unwrapping. Cut each half into 5 slices, and cut each slice into 4 pieces. Drop each piece into a greased mini-muffin cup. Bake according to package directions, or until golden brown. Press a peanut butter candy into each cookie as soon as they come out of the oven. When chocolate starts to melt slightly, sprinkle with chopped pecans. When completely cool, remove from pans.

Mom's Chocolate Roll

Nancy Tomsen

4 egg whites
4 egg yolks
1/3 c. flour
1/4 c. cocoa
lightly sweetened whipped cream

1 t. vanilla
2/3 c. sugar
1/4 t. salt
1/2 t. baking powder

Beat egg whites until peaks form. Add sugar gradually. Continue beating until well mixed. Beat egg yolks until thick, then add vanilla. Sift flour, salt, cocoa and baking powder together. Combine yolks and whites and fold into flour mixture. Bake on waxed paper lined cookie sheet at 350 degrees for 12 minutes. Remove paper and trim crust. Roll up in a tea towel sprinkled with powdered sugar. Cool. Unroll and fill with lightly sweetened whipped cream. Roll again. Serve with chocolate sauce.

Chocolate Sauce:
1 c. sugar
1 c. milk
2 T. cocoa

pinch of salt
1 1/2 T. flour
1 t. vanilla

Cook sugar, milk, cocoa, salt and flour until slightly thickened. Add vanilla and a lump of butter.

Dump Cake

Janie Milum

1 can pie filling, plus 1 can same
    kind fruit, drained
1 medium size can crushed pineapple
1 box white or yellow cake mix

1 stick butter, melted
pecans
coconut

Put pie filling and fruit in 13" x 9" pan. Add pineapple, then spread dry cake mix over top. Pour butter over the cake mix and sprinkle with pecans. Bake at 350 degrees for 35 minutes. Sprinkle with coconut and bake for another 10 minutes.

Mexican Fruitcake

Florence Rainey

2 c. flour
2 c. sugar
20 oz. can unsweetened crushed
    pineapple (do not drain)

1 c. pecans, finely chopped
2 eggs, beaten
2 t. baking soda

Preheat oven to 350 degrees. Combine all ingredients in a mixer bowl and blend well. Spread batter into a greased and floured 9" x 13" pan. Bake for 1 hour. Frost while hot.

Cream Cheese Frosting:
8 oz. cream cheese, softened
2 to 2 1/2 c. powdered sugar

1 t. vanilla

Combine all ingredients and beat until smooth. Spread frosting over hot cake.

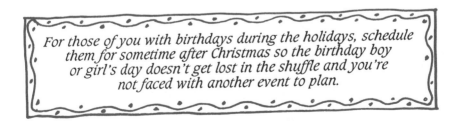

For those of you with birthdays during the holidays, schedule them for sometime after Christmas so the birthday boy or girl's day doesn't get lost in the shuffle and you're not faced with another event to plan.

Cherries In the Snow
Linda Brody

1/3 c. margarine, melted
3/4 c. confectioners sugar
1 t. almond extract
2 c. (1 lb. 6 oz. can) cherry pie filling
1 1/4 c. graham cracker crumbs
    or pie crust

8 oz. cream cheese, softened
1 T. milk
1/2 c. chopped pecans
1 carton frozen whipped
    topping

Combine crumbs and margarine. Press into a 9" pan, or buy a graham cracker crust. Mix cream cheese, sugar and 1/2 teaspoon almond extract. Mix well. Spread on crust, and sprinkle with nuts. Spread whipped topping over nuts. Combine cherry pie filling and the rest of the almond extract and spread over whipped topping. Chill.

Brandy Raisins
Dorothy Hanford

An "Olde" English Christmas Eve tradition dating to the 1870's.

seedless raisins

brandy

Put raisins in a pretty fire-proof dish. Pour brandy over them and set afire. Burn for a few seconds, blow out fire and enjoy the "tid-bits." Yum!

Sonia's Mexican Wedding Cookies
Sonia Bracamonte

2 1/2 c. flour
3/4 c. powdered sugar
pinch of anise, if desired

1 c. butter
1 1/2 t. vanilla
1/4 t. salt

Cream butter, and add remaining ingredients. Mix until you have a stiff dough. Chill in refrigerator for 3 hours. Roll into balls about 1" in diameter, and bake on a greased cookie sheet at 350 degrees for 10 to 12 minutes. When almost cooled, roll in powdered sugar. When ready to serve, roll in powdered sugar again.

Grandma Dixon's Applespice Cake

Alison Johnson

2 1/2 c. flour
1 t. salt
3/4 t. ground nutmeg
1/4 t. baking powder
1 1/2 c. sugar
16 oz. applesauce

1 1/2 t. baking soda
1 t. ground cinnamon
1/2 t. ground cloves
1/2 c. butter
2 eggs
1/2 c. walnuts, chopped

Grease and flour a 13" x 9" x 2" pan. Combine flour, baking soda, salt, cinnamon, nutmeg, cloves and baking powder in a medium bowl. Use electric mixer to beat butter, then cream in sugar. Add each egg, beating for 1 minute after each. Add all the dry ingredients and the applesauce with mixer on low. Stir in walnuts. Bake at 350 degrees for 45 minutes. Turn out onto a wire rack to cool. Wrap in foil or colored plastic wrap and tie with Christmas ribbon.

Pumpkin Fruitcake

Karen Mauger

29 oz. can pumpkin
4 c. sugar
5 c. flour
1 t. ground cloves
1 t. ground cinnamon
2 c. candied cherries, cut in quarters

1 c. oil
4 t. baking soda
1 t. ground ginger
1 t. salt
2 c. chopped walnuts
2 c. raisins

Mix pumpkin, oil and sugar in a large bowl. Sift together flour, baking soda, cloves, ginger, cinnamon and salt. Stir in raisins, walnuts and candied cherries. Distribute batter evenly in greased 8" x 5" x 2 1/2" loaf pans. Bake at 350 degrees for 50 to 60 minutes or until cake starts to pull away from sides of pan. Cool for 10 minutes, then remove to a cooling rack. Wrap tightly and store. The fruitcake keeps well in the refrigerator and can be frozen. Makes 8 miniature loaves.

Cheesecake Cupcakes
Darlene Lucas

3-8 oz. pkgs. cream cheese
1/2 t. vanilla

5 eggs
1 c. sugar

Preheat oven to 350 degrees. Blend all the ingredients together with electric mixer. Pour into cupcake papers, in cupcake tins, 3/4 full. Bake for 25 minutes, remove from oven and let tops fall.

1 c. sour cream
1/4 c. sugar

1/4 t. vanilla

Mix ingredients together. Spoon 1 teaspoon into each dip in top of cupcake. Bake for 5 minutes. Top with your favorite preserves, if desired. Store in an airtight container in the refrigerator. Makes 28 cupcakes.

Peanut Butter Bars
Anna Leon-Guerrero

1 stick margarine
1 1/2 c. peanut butter
   (chunky or smooth)

3 c. powdered sugar
4 T. butter
12 oz. chocolate chips

Blend together with a fork the margarine, peanut butter and powdered sugar. Pat into a 9" x 9" pan. Melt the chocolate chips and butter together in a double-boiler. Spread chocolate onto the peanut butter mixture. Refrigerate. Cut into serving portions.

Molasses Roll Out Cookies By Mabel Dick
Marcia Carlson

1 c. sour cream
1 heaping t. baking soda
1 t. or less of ginger
4 c. flour (may need more)

1 egg
1 c. butter (oleo)
1 c. sugar
1 c. molasses

Mix together to make a soft dough. Chill about 3 hours. Roll out and cut. Bake at 400 degrees for about 12 minutes. Frost if desired.

Chocolate Caramels
By Esther Carlson

Marcia Carlson

2 c. sugar
1 3/4 c. white corn syrup
1 c. butter
1 c. nuts (we use black walnuts)

1 c. cream
1 c. rich milk
4 T. cocoa
1 t. vanilla

Cook the sugar, syrup, butter and cocoa until mixture boils vigorously. Gradually add the cream and milk, but do not let boiling stop. Boil to the hard ball stage or 250 degrees. Remove from fire, add nuts and vanilla. Pour on marble or into a buttered glass pan. DO NOT MAKE ON DAMP DAYS. We have in recent years substituted canned evaporated milk for the cream and milk and oleo for the butter. They work well.

Chocolate-Banana Bread

Helen Overstreet

1/2 c. butter, softened
2 eggs
2 T. cocoa
1 t. salt
1 t. vanilla extract
1/2 c. sour cream
1/3 to 1/2 c. miniature semi-sweet
    chocolate morsels

1 c. sugar
1 1/2 c. flour
1 t. baking soda
1/2 t. ground cinnamon
1 c. ripe banana, mashed
1/2 c. pecans

Cream butter; gradually add sugar. Beat until light and fluffy. Add eggs, one at a time, beating well after each egg. Sift together in a small bowl the flour, cocoa, baking soda, salt and cinnamon. Stir flour mixture into egg mixture, blending well. Add vanilla. Stir in banana, sour cream, pecans and chocolate morsels. Spoon batter into 2 greased and floured 7 1/2" x 3" x 2" loaf pans. Bake at 350 degrees for 55 minutes or until toothpick inserted in center comes out clean. Cool in pans for 15 minutes on wire racks. Remove from pans and cool on wire racks. Makes 2 loaves.

Decorate a tree with cookies! Gnomes, heart in hands or gingerbread men look great and smell delicious.

The Christmas Groaning Board

Hot Roll Cookies
Aileen Roberts

1 box hot roll mix   oil

Heat oil, but not too hot (just so it bubbles a piece of dough). Prepare hot roll mix. Lightly flour a bread board. After roll mix has raised, gently roll out mix to fit your cookie cutter, 1 1/2 to 2 inches thick. Cut out shapes. Brush away as much flour as possible. Then fry both sides of cookie. Serve hot with colored sugar. Add a glass of milk and a baked apple—so good!

Orange Pudding Cake
Sharon Perry

1 pkg. (2-layer) orange cake mix   4 eggs
1 pkg. (4-serving) instant vanilla   1 c. water
       pudding mix   1/4 c. oil

Combine all ingredients in a large mixing bowl. Blend, then beat for 2 minutes. Pour into a greased and floured 10" bundt or tube pan. Bake at 350 degrees for 50 minutes. Cool 15 minutes then remove from pan.

Frosting:
1 c. confectioners sugar   2 T. orange juice

Mix ingredients together and then drizzle frosting over cake.

Lemon Sauce
Linda Kirchner

2 c. hot water   1 c. sugar
1 lemon, juice and rind   2 T. cornstarch
2 T. butter

Mix the sugar and cornstarch, add boiling water gradually, stirring all the time. Cook 8 to 10 minutes. Add lemon juice and butter. Serve hot.

Amish White Cookies
Patsy Grimmett

1 c. sugar
1 c. butter, softened
2 eggs
1 T. vanilla
1 t. baking soda

1 c. powdered sugar
1 c. vegetable oil
1/2 t. salt
4 1/2 c. flour
1 t. cream of tartar

Cream together in a bowl the sugars, butter, oil, eggs, salt and vanilla. Set aside. In a large bowl sift together the flour, baking soda and tartar. Add the sugar and butter mixture to dry ingredients. Mix well. Cover and chill for several hours (3 or more). After dough is thoroughly chilled, separate into smaller balls and roll to 1/4" thickness on a floured board. (Keep the rest of the dough as cool as possible.) Cut into desired shapes and bake on an ungreased cookie sheet at 350 degrees for 12 minutes or until bottom of cookie is lightly brown. Makes approximately 2 to 3 dozen.

Rolled Diabetic Sugar Cookies
Kimberly Burns

1/2 c. sugar
6 pkgs. "Sweet One" (do not use any
     other brand)
1 egg
1 c. butter or margarine, softened
1/2 t. salt

3 T. milk
1 t. vanilla
3 c. flour
1/2 t. baking powder

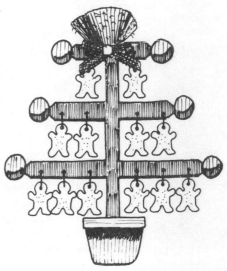

In a large bowl, combine sugar, sweetener, milk, vanilla, egg and butter or margarine. Blend well. Stir in remaining ingredients, blend well. Chill dough for 2 hours or overnight. Roll out on a floured surface. Use floured cookie cutters. Bake at 400 degrees for 5 to 6 minutes. Remove from cookie sheet immediately. These may be frosted with or without a sugar-reduced frosting, if desired. They taste great plain too. Makes about 2 dozen large cookies.

Persimmon Pudding

Ramona Mullins

1 1/2 c. sugar
1/2 c. margarine
3 eggs
1 t. baking soda
2 t. spices (combination of allspice,
   clove, and cinnamon)

1 c. flour, sifted
2 c. milk
1 t. salt
1 t. baking powder
1 pt. persimmon pulp

Rub persimmons through colander to remove the seeds. Beat eggs well and add to pulp. Add flour and other dry ingredients. Add milk slowly, stirring the mixture well. Put the margarine into a baking dish in the oven as oven is preheating to the baking temperature of 350 degrees. Pour excess margarine into the pudding mixture and continue stirring until smooth. Bake approximately 1 hour. Pudding will turn dark from the spices as it is baking. Pudding is delicious served with a dollop of frozen whipped topping or with ice cream.

Christmas Day Decoration Dessert

Katherine Wienberg

1/2 stick margarine or butter
8 oz. cream cheese
2 pkg. french vanilla pudding
    (not jumbo)
1 large pkg. chocolate sandwich
    cookies, crushed (approximately 1 1/4 lb.)

3 1/2 c. milk
1 large container frozen
    whipped topping
1 c. powdered sugar

Blend together all ingredients, except the cookies. Layer in a large clay pot, pudding mixture, then cookies. Start with cookies and end with cookies for topping. Add plastic poinsettia flowers to "grow" in the pot, and a festive bow on the pot. Every year we have fun eating our "centerpiece."

Orange Slice Cake

Ramona Mullins

3 1/2 c. flour
1 lb. orange slice candy (cut into
    small pieces)
8 oz. pkg. dates (cut into small
    pieces)

1/2 t. salt
2 c. walnuts, chopped
1 to 3 3/4 oz. coconut

Combine orange slices, dates, walnuts and coconut. Add 1/2 cup of the 3 1/2 cups flour to the mixture and mix well.

1 c. margarine
4 eggs
1/2 c. buttermilk
2 c. powdered sugar

2 c. sugar
1 t. baking soda
1 c. orange juice

Cream margarine and sugar, then add the eggs. Mix the baking soda into the buttermilk. Combine remaining flour with the salt, and add alternately with the buttermilk mixture and the margarine mixture. When all are blended, then add the candy mixture. Put into a greased and floured tube pan. Bake at 300 degrees for 1 hour and 45 minutes. Remove cake from oven. Combine the orange juice and powdered sugar and pour mixture over hot cake. Cool, then refrigerate overnight. Remove from pan and enjoy.

The Christmas Groaning Board

Cherry Cheese Cups
Kathy McFarlane

8 oz. cream cheese   2 sticks butter
2 c. flour

Blend ingredients together to make a dough. Roll dough thin and make small balls (approximately 72). Put each in a miniature muffin pan and make small cups. Bake at 350 degrees for 15 minutes.

FILLING:
8 oz. cream cheese, softened   1/3 c. lemon juice
1 can sweetened condensed milk   1 t. vanilla
cherry pie filling

Beat ingredients at medium speed until thickened. Fill cups 3/4 full with mixture. Top with cherry pie filling. Chill for 2 hours before serving.

Santa's Cookies
Barbara Heck

Serve these cookies with hot chocolate on Christmas Eve, but be sure to leave Santa his share!

1 c. butter, melted   2 T. powdered sugar
2 c. flour   splash vanilla
1/2 c. pecans, chopped

Mix all ingredients well. Form into small balls. Place balls on ungreased cookie sheet and flatten. Place in preheated 300 degree oven and bake for 30 minutes, or until slightly brown. Do not overbake. Dust with powdered sugar while hot. When cooled, dust again.

Sour Cream Cookies

Susie Garber

3 eggs
1 level t. baking soda
5 or more full c. flour

2 c. sugar
1/2 c. butter
1 c. sour cream

Mix all the ingredients together into a dough. Roll onto a floured surface and cut into Christmas shapes. Bake at 350 degrees for approximately 10 minutes.

Cut-Out Cookies

Barbara Loe

2 1/2 c. flour
1 1/4 c. sugar
3/4 c. (1 1/2 sticks) butter or
    margarine

1/2 t. salt
1 egg
2 t. vanilla

Beat butter, sugar and egg in large mixer bowl at high speed for 3 minutes, or until fluffy. Blend in vanilla. Stir in flour and salt to make a stiff dough. Wrap in waxed paper and chill for 3 hours, or until firm enough to roll. Roll dough, 1/4 at a time, to a 1/4" thickness on a lightly floured surface. Place 1" apart on ungreased cookie sheets. Sprinkle with colored sugars, if desired. Bake at 350 degrees for 8 minutes, or until lightly browned at edges. Cool on wire racks. These cut-outs stay crisp very well and they freeze very well. The flavor improves as they age. Yields 3 dozen.

Icing:
powdered sugar
drops of water

food colorings

Combine ingredients until you reach the consistency desired. Use paint-brushes (like for watercolors) and paint cookies when cool.

165

Gramma's Snappiest Ever Ginger Snap Cookies
Karen Roberts

3/4 c. shortening
2 t. baking soda
1 c. sugar
4 T. molasses
1 egg

2 c. flour, sifted
1 t. ginger
1 t. cloves
1 t. cinnamon

Cream shortening. Add sugar, molasses and egg. Beat well and add sifted dry ingredients. Beat until smooth. Mixture will be very stiff. Take a teaspoonful of mixture, roll into a ball, then roll ball in bowl of sugar. Bake on a greased cookie sheet at 350 degrees for 10 to 12 minutes.

School Cookies
Dena Cardi

4 c. sugar
6 T. unsweetened cocoa
2/3 c. evaporated milk
1 heaping c. peanut butter

1 c. butter
1/3 c. water
6 c. oats
2 t. vanilla

In a large saucepan, mix together sugar, butter, cocoa, water and evaporated milk. Cook, stirring often, until mixture comes to a boil (about 20 minutes). Boil for about 4 minutes. In a large bowl, mix oats and peanut butter. Add cooked mixture and stir in the vanilla, mixing well. Working quickly, drop by spoonfuls onto waxed paper and allow to sit overnight. Makes about 5 dozen. NOTE: Mix and drop cookies quickly, if the mixture cools too much it will crumble before you can shape them.

Apple Dessert
LaVerne Biunno

apples, pared and quartered
1/2 c. sugar
2 c. warm water

2 T. flour
dash of salt
nutmeg

Pare and quarter enough apples to make 2 layers in a pan or a baking dish. Mix flour, sugar, salt and water together. Pour over apples enough to cover them. Sprinkle nutmeg over the top and bake until soft about 30 minutes in 350 degree oven. Serve warm with pork dishes or cold with cream for dessert.

Pistachio Whip
LaVerne Biunno

2 pkg. pistachio instant pudding
2-16 oz. cans pineapple tidbits
    and juice

2-12 oz. cartons frozen
    whipped topping

Combine whipped topping and pineapple juice together well. Add pistachio pudding and mix well. Add pineapple and mix well. Very light and re-freshing.

Lemon Butter Cookies
Marlene Wetzel

1/2 c. sugar
3/4 c. butter or margarine, softened
1 T. grated lemon peel
1 egg
1/2 t. cream of tartar
yellow decorator sugar

1/2 c. powdered sugar
1/4 c. oil
1 T. lemon juice
2 1/2 c. flour
1/2 t. baking soda
1/4 t. salt

In a bowl, beat sugar, powdered sugar, butter and oil until light and fluffy. Add lemon peel, lemon juice and egg, blending well. Stir in flour, cream of tartar, baking soda and salt, mixing well. Cover with plastic wrap and refrigerate for 1 hour. Preheat oven to 350 degrees. Shape dough into 1" balls. Roll in decorator sugar. Place 2" apart on an ungreased cookie sheet and bake for 7 to 12 minutes, or until set. Remove cookies from sheet. Makes 3 1/2 dozen cookies.

The Christmas Groaning Board

Frosted Snow Squares
Marilyn Rokahr

1 envelope gelatin
1 c. boiling water
3 egg whites, unbeaten
13 graham crackers (rolled very fine)

4 T. cold water
3/4 c. granulated sugar
1/4 t. salt
1 t. vanilla

Sprinkle gelatin over cold water. Soak 5 minutes. Add boiling water and stir until dissolved. Let cool. MUST be cold before adding egg whites. Add egg whites, sugar, salt and vanilla. Beat at high speed until light and thick. This takes time and will look like marshmallow when done. Turn into a 9" x 9" x 2" pan. Chill in refrigerator for several hours. Cut in squares. Remove from tin and roll in cracker crumbs. Serve with lemon sauce.

Lemon Sauce:
3 egg yolks
1/3 c. butter, melted
1 T. real lemon juice

1/3 c. sugar
1/3 c. whipping cream

Beat yolks until light. Add sugar gradually. Continue beating, adding butter and lemon juice. Beat in cream, being careful not to beat cream too stiff. May be kept in the refrigerator until ready to serve.

Candy Balls
Diane Dollak

2 c. graham cracker crumbs
6 oz. pkg. chopped, mixed dried
  fruit bits

1 c. pecans, chopped
14 oz. can sweetened
  condensed milk

Mix well with a spoon or hands. Roll into balls the size of cherries. Store in the refrigerator with a sheet of waxed paper between each layer.

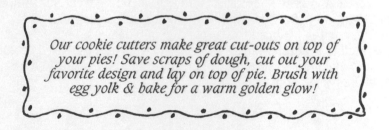

Our cookie cutters make great cut-outs on top of your pies! Save scraps of dough, cut out your favorite design and lay on top of pie. Brush with egg yolk & bake for a warm golden glow!

Gingerbread Men

Julie Zadra

1/4 c. boiling water
1 t. baking soda
1 t. cinnamon
1 t. ginger
1/2 c. baking molasses
3 c. flour

1/2 c. butter
1/2 t. salt
1/4 t. ground cloves
1 egg
1/2 c. brown sugar

Melt butter in boiling water. Add all the other ingredients. Then chill the dough for 2 hours. Roll out and cut into shapes. Bake at 350 degrees for 8 to 10 minutes. Cool and decorate with frosting or decorate with raisins before baking. Makes 24 cookies.

Strawberry Pockets

Michelle Cione

8 oz. cream cheese, softened
2 c. all-purpose flour
1/2 c. strawberry preserves
    (any preserves can be used)

1 c. margarine
confectioners sugar

Combine cream cheese and margarine. Mix until well blended. Add flour, mix well. On a lightly floured surface, roll out dough to 1/8" thickness. Cut with a 2 1/2" round cookie cutter. Place on a cookie sheet. Place 1/4 teaspoon of preserves in the center of each circle. Moisten edges with cold water. Fold in half, seal edges. Bake at 375 degrees for 14 to 16 minutes, or until lightly browned. Sprinkle with confectioners sugar. MAKE AHEAD: Prepare as above, omitting the confectioners sugar. Wrap securely and freeze. When ready to serve, thaw unwrapped at room temperature for about 2 hours. Sprinkle with confectioners sugar. Makes 3 1/2 dozen.

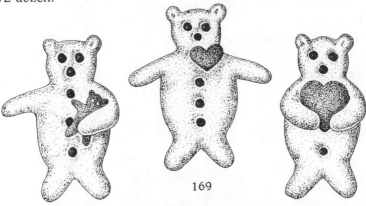

Ricotta Cheese Cookies

Michelle Cione

3 eggs
2 c. sugar
1 t. vanilla
4 c. all-purpose flour

1/2 lb. butter
1 lb. ricotta cheese
1 t. salt
1 t. baking soda

Cream sugar and butter. Add eggs, ricotta cheese and vanilla; mix. Add dry ingredients, mix well. Drop by teaspoon onto a greased cookie sheet. Bake at 375 degrees for 10 minutes, then frost.

Frosting:
1/2 c. (1 stick) margarine
1 box confectioners sugar

2 t. vegetable shortening
1/2 t. vanilla

Beat margarine, add shortening and mix. Add sugar and vanilla; mix, adding a few drops of milk to help blend. Cookies may be sprinkled with colored sugar right after being frosted. Makes 10 dozen.

Spritz Cookies

Leslie Deatrich

Whenever I used to make Spritz cookies in past years, I always had leftover egg whites (the recipe requires egg yolks only). I hated to throw them away. Then my friend suggested that I make Forgotten Cookies (also known as Sleeping Cookies, see page 171.) This recipe requires egg whites only; therefore I ended up with more cookies and no more wasted ingredients.

1 c. butter, softened
3 egg yolks
1/8 t. salt

3/4 c. sugar
1 t. vanilla
2 1/4 c. flour

Cream butter and sugar until light and fluffy. Add egg yolks, vanilla and salt; beat well. Add flour gradually; dough will be stiff. Fill cookie press; place cookies on an ungreased cookie sheet. Bake at 400 degrees for 8 to 10 minutes.

Forgotten Cookies

Leslie Deatrich

3 egg whites
1 c. sugar
8 oz. miniature chocolate chips

3/8 t. salt
1 1/2 t. vanilla

Preheat oven to 375 degrees. Beat egg whites with salt until stiff. Slowly add sugar and vanilla. Fold in chocolate chips. Drop onto a greased cookie sheet. Put in oven, turn oven off and leave overnight.

Joyful Jade Cream

Marsha Richards

1 qt. vanilla ice cream, softened
1/4 c. creme de menthe syrup

1 pt. lime sherbet
1 pkg. whipped topping mix

Prepare topping mix according to directions. Add softened ice cream, sherbet and creme de menthe. Mix thoroughly. Put into containers and freeze. Serve with chocolate sauce.

Another serving suggestion: Using individual bowls or parfaits, cover bottom with chocolate or vanilla cookie crumbs, add softened Jade Cream, then freeze. Garnish before serving with sauce, curls, leaves or even a mint leaf.

Sugar Cookie Cut-Outs

Martha Terrell

batch of sugar cookies
brightly colored sugar crystal

homemade cut-outs

Before you bake, cover a sugar cookie with a small homemade paper cut-out (heart, star, etc.) Sprinkle sugar crystals over your cut-out to "stencil" on your own design.

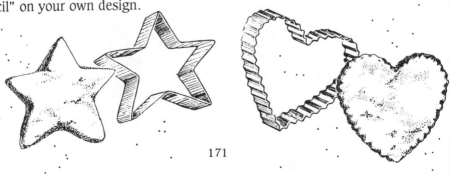

Nantucket Cranberry Crisp

Donna Weidner

Filling:
6 c. frozen cranberry or other fruit   1/2 c. sugar
1/2 c. walnuts, chopped

Frosting:
2 eggs, beaten   1/2 c. sugar
1/2 c. flour

Butter a shallow ceramic pan, pour filling in, top with topping. Bake at 350 degrees for 30 to 40 minutes, until glossy and crisp.

Peppermint Candy Ice Cream Pie

Mimi Shanahan

1 1/2 c. chocolate wafer crumbs   1 pt. peppermint ice cream
1/4 c. plus 2 T. butter or margarine,   8 oz. frozen whipped topping
    melted   (partially thawed)
3 T. peppermint candy, finely   Additional peppermint
    crushed   candy, for garnish

Combine crumbs and melted butter; press firmly into a 9" pie plate. Combine peppermint ice cream and whipped topping; spoon into crumb crust. Sprinkle with peppermint candy; freeze until firm. Garnish with peppermint candy, if desired. Makes 1-9" pie.

Fruity Cookie Recipe

Leigh Vaughn

Use strawberry and lime gelatin to get the red and green Christmas colors.

4 c. all-purpose flour, sifted
1 t. double-acting baking powder
3 oz. pkg. gelatin, any flavor
additional gelatin

1 1/2 c. butter
1 c. sugar
1 egg
1 t. vanilla

Sift flour with baking powder. Cream butter. Gradually add sugar and gelatin, cream well after each addition. Add egg and vanilla; beat well. Gradually add flour mixture, mixing after each addition until smooth. Force dough through cookie press onto ungreased baking sheets. Sprinkle with gelatin. Decorate as desired. Bake at 375 degrees about 9 or 10 minutes, or until golden brown at edges. Store in loosely covered container. Makes about 5 dozen cookies.

Oatmeal Cookies

Doris Allen

1 c. shortening
3 eggs
1 T. vanilla
3 c. flour
2 t. cinnamon
1/4 t. salt
1 t. baking powder

2 c. brown sugar
3 T. cream
4 T. sorghum (molasses)
1 to 2 t. cloves
1 t. nutmeg
1 t. baking soda
1 1/2 c. oatmeal

Mix together shortening and brown sugar. Add eggs, cream, vanilla, and sorghum. Sift together and then add flour, cloves, cinnamon, nutmeg, salt, baking soda and baking powder. Add the oatmeal last. Mix together and bake at 350 degrees for 8 minutes. Variations that can be used include: 1 cup of dates, nuts, or raisins, 1/2 cup coconut, grated orange rind, etc.

Chocolate Christmas Balls

Debbie Lloyd

3/4 c. sweetened condensed milk
12 oz. chocolate chips

1 c. walnuts, chopped
1 t. vanilla

Melt chocolate in a double-boiler. Remove. Add all the other ingredients. Mix and cool in refrigerator for 10 minutes. Roll into balls. Then roll in toppings of your choice. Topping suggestions: coconut, nuts, non-pareils, candy sprinkles.

Peg's Pretzel Dessert

Peg Buckingham

Crust:
9 oz. bag pretzels, crushed
(salted or unsalted)
1 1/2 sticks margarine, melted

3 T. sugar

Mix together and press into the bottom of a 9" x 13" casserole dish. Bake at 350 degrees for 10 minutes. Cool.

Filling:
8 oz. pkg. cream cheese, softened
1 medium-size frozen whipped topping

1 c. sugar

Beat cheese and sugar together and fold in whipped topping. Spread over crust and chill.

Topping:
6 oz. strawberry gelatin
16 oz. pkg. frozen sliced strawberries

2 c. boiling water
1 c. cold water

Dissolve gelatin in boiling water; add cold water and frozen strawberries. Let set until it begins to gel; then spoon over cheese layer and chill.

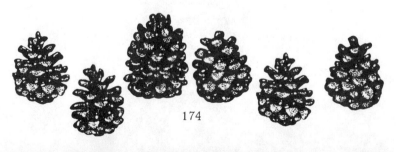

Christmas Sandies
Debra Himes

1 c. butter or margarine
2 t. vanilla
1 c. walnuts or pecans, chopped

1/4 c. powdered sugar
1 T. water
2 c. flour

Cream butter or margarine and sugar together. Add vanilla, water and nuts. Add flour and mix well. Bake at 300 degrees for 25 to 30 minutes. Roll in powdered sugar when still a little warm, so it sticks to the cookies. Makes 2 dozen.

Old-Fashioned Shortcake
Susan Kirschenheiter

2 c. flour
1 T. baking powder
1/2 c. margarine

1/4 c. sugar
1/2 t. salt
3/4 c. milk

Preheat oven to 450 degrees. Lightly grease an 8" x 8" x 2" pan. Mix flour, sugar, baking powder and salt. With pastry blender, cut in the margarine. Make well in center and pour in milk. Mix quickly with a fork, just to moisten. Turn into pan. Bake for 15 minutes or until done and lightly browned.

ThE ChRiSTmAS GRoaNiNg BoaRd

New Year's Cakes
Susan Kirschenheiter

2 eggs, beaten
1/3 c. margarine, melted
4 c. flour
1 t. baking soda
1 t. nutmeg

1 c. sugar
1 c. milk
3 t. baking powder
1 t. salt

Combine in a bowl the eggs, sugar and margarine. Add the milk. Combine in another bowl the flour, baking powder, soda, salt and nutmeg. Mix the dry ingredients with the liquid ingredients. Roll on a lightly floured board until 1" thick. Cut into strips a little longer than your fingers. Place on a cookie sheet in the shape of an "S." The less you handle the dough, the better your results. Bake at 375 to 400 degrees until lightly browned.

Frosting:
1/2 box powdered sugar
cold milk (to thin)

2 T. margarine, melted

Mix all the ingredients with an electric mixer. Frost cakes and sprinkle with colored sugar.

Cherry Nothings
Susan Kirschenheiter

2 sticks margarine
4 eggs
1 can cherry pie filling

1 1/2 c. sugar
2 c. flour

Beat margarine, sugar and eggs at high speed and add flour. Mix well. Grease a large cookie sheet that has sides. Mark off squares in batter after putting it in the cookie sheet, and make indentations in each square with a spoon tip. Put a cherry in each indentation. Bake at 350 degrees for 20 to 30 minutes. Drizzle on a glaze when cooled and cut into squares.

Glaze:
small amount of milk

powdered sugar

Combine ingredients to desired thickness and drizzle on Cherry Nothings.

Soft Gingerbread

Tricia Collings

1/2 c. sugar (white and brown mixed)
1/2 c. shortening
1 t. ginger
2 t. baking soda, dissolved in 1 c.
    boiling water

1 c. sorghum molasses
1 t. cinnamon
2 1/2 c. flour
2 eggs, well beaten

Mix all ingredients except the eggs, then add them just before baking.
Bake at 350 degrees for 45 minutes or until done.

Fruit Cake Cookies

Linda Crowley

1/4 lb. butter
3 eggs
1/4 c. bourbon or whiskey
1/2 lb. candied cherries
2 t. vanilla
1/2 lb. candied pineapple
4 c. chopped pecans

1/2 c. plus 1 T. sugar
1 1/4 c. self-rising flour
1/4 t. allspice
1/4 t. salt
1/4 t. cloves
1/4 t. cinnamon

Cut up fruit and soak it in whiskey,
while getting other ingredients ready.
Cream butter and sugar and add eggs.
Mix dry ingredients together and add
to creamed mixture. Add the fruit. Add
vanilla and nuts last. If batter seems
too thin, add 2 tablespoons of flour.
Bake at 250 degrees for 25 to 30
minutes, until light brown. Do not
overcook.

The Christmas Groaning Board

Grandmother's Christmas Pie

L.H. Barclay

1 unbaked pie shell
pumpkin filling

mincemeat
whipped cream

In an unbaked pie shell, put a layer of mincemeat. Then pour pumpkin filling on top and bake according to pie filling directions. Serve warm with whipped cream.

Rotterdam Banket

Ann Mers

4 c. flour
1 lb. margarine, softened
2 c. sugar
3 eggs, beaten (save a
   little white for the top)

1/2 t. baking powder
1 c. ice water
1 lb. almond paste

Mix together the flour, baking powder, margarine and water, chill in refrigerator over night. Combine eggs, sugar and almond paste to make filling. Mix with your fingers and divide into 8 pieces. Set in refrigerator for 24 hours. Roll pie mixture 1/8" thick into 8 strips. Fill with almond mixture. Roll up and seal ends and edges; brush with remaining egg white. Slit with knife every 2". Bake at 450 degrees for 20 minutes, until brown. Makes 8 rolls.

Christmas Popcorn Trees

Sandi Cargill

sugar ice cream cones
popcorn

green frosting
red cinnamon candies

Cover sugar ice cream cones with tinted green frosting. While icing is still soft, press and cover with popcorn, then dot with red cinnamon candies. Makes an adorable, edible Christmas tree.

Icing:
1 egg white
1 1/2 T. water

2 1/2 c. powdered sugar
6 drops green food coloring

Mix ingredients together, follow directions above, and enjoy!

Baklava

Sally Gorby

This recipe was given to me several years ago by a very special Greek lady friend of my grandmother's.

1 pkg. frozen phyllo dough
1 lb. nuts (I use 1/2 c. English
    walnuts and 1/2 c. pecans)
1 stick butter, melted (or more if
    necessary)

1/4 t. nutmeg
1 t. cinnamon
1 c. white sugar

Set phyllo dough in the refrigerator to thaw, making sure to keep it completely wrapped so it does not dry out. Mix nuts and spices in a small mixing bowl with fork. GENTLY unwrap phyllo dough. Keep covered with a damp towel while working with it, so that it stays moist. Dough will tear easily if it dries out. Butter a glass baking dish at least 9" x 13" in size. Preheat oven to 300 degrees. Layer phyllo dough in sets of two sheets, buttering between each layer of two sheets, for twelve sheets (or six layers.) Sprinkle out nut mixture over dough just to cover all of dough, do not overload the nuts. Add two more sheets of phyllo, cover with melted butter, then nuts; add two more sheets of phyllo and repeat until all of the nut mixture is used. Then layer two sheets of phyllo, buttering between each two, until you make six more layers. Using an electric knife, cut into 1" squares and sprinkle lightly with cold water. Bake in oven for 1 hour, or until golden brown on top. While dough is baking, prepare syrup.

Syrup:
1 cinnamon stick (do not use
    ground cinnamon)
2 globs (close your eyes and
    spoon some out) of honey

2 c. white sugar
2 c. water
1 t. lemon juice

Combine sugar, water, lemon juice and cinnamon stick in large saucepan. Cook for 15 minutes, then add the two globs of honey. Keep stirring throughout. Pour syrup immediately over the dough when it comes out of the oven, reserving the cinnamon stick for future use, or for crafting. (It will seem as if you are completely drowning the dough, but it will all soak in.) Don't cover the dish until completely cool, or you will have "wrinkled" Baklava.

Chocolate Frosted Ice Cream Roll   *Anne Legan*

1/2 c. flour	1/2 t. vanilla
1/3 c. cocoa	1/4 t. almond extract
1 qt. vanilla ice cream, softened	1 t. baking powder
1/4 t. salt	3/4 c. sugar
4 eggs, separated (room temp)	nuts (optional)
chocolate frosting	

Grease a 15" x 10" x 1" jelly roll pan. Line pan with waxed paper, grease pan and top of paper. Beat egg whites at HIGH speed until foamy. Gradually add sugar, beating until soft peaks form, then set aside. Sift together the flour, cocoa, baking powder and salt. Beat egg yolks until thick and lemon colored, stir in flavorings. Fold yolks into egg whites, then gently fold in flour mixture. Spread evenly in prepared pan. Bake at 350 degrees for 12 minutes. When cake is done, immediately loosen from sides of pan, and turn out onto a towel covered with powdered sugar. Peel off the waxed paper. Starting at the wide end, roll up cake and towel together. Let cool on a wire rack, seam side down for about 30 minutes. Unroll the cake, remove the towel, and spread softened ice cream evenly over cake. Gently roll cake back up, and carefully place on a large baking sheet. Freeze until firm. Frost cake with chocolate frosting and freeze until serving time.

Chocolate Frosting:

1/4 c. butter	3 T. milk
2 c. powdered sugar, sifted	3 T. cocoa
1 t. vanilla	

Combine ingredients, beat until smooth. Frost top and sides of ice cream cake. Yield: Enough frosting for cake roll.

The Christmas PANTRY

to: JoAnn
from: Vickie

The Christmas Groaning Board

Five Minute Fudge
Adel Bennett

1 1/2 c. small marshmallows
1 to 1 1/2 c. small semi-sweet bits
2/3 c. undiluted evaporated milk

1 2/3 c. sugar
1 t. vanilla

Combine sugar and milk in a saucepan. Heat to boiling and cook for 5 minutes, stirring constantly. Remove from heat and add the other ingredients. Stir until marshmallows and chocolate bits are melted. Pour into buttered 8" or 9" pan.

Peanut Brittle
Margaret Reynolds

2 c. sugar
1 T. butter

1/2 t. baking soda
1 can cocktail peanuts

Cook sugar over slow heat until caramelized. Remove from heat and add baking soda and butter. As it foams, stir in peanuts. Pour into a greased pan to cool. Break into small pieces.

Bread and Butter Pickles
Bonnie Jennings

8 or 9 medium cucumbers
5 or 6 medium onions
2 green peppers
1 clove garlic
2 T. pickling spice

1/3 c. salt
5 c. sugar
3 c. cider vinegar
1 1/2 t. tumeric

Cut cucumbers, peppers and garlic into a bowl, add salt. Let stand for 3 hours. Bring remaining ingredients to a boil in a pot. Add drained cucumbers and bring again to a boil. Put into quart or pint jars. Makes 4 1/2 quarts.

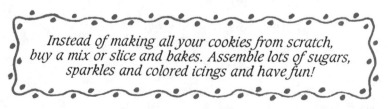

Instead of making all your cookies from scratch, buy a mix or slice and bakes. Assemble lots of sugars, sparkles and colored icings and have fun!

Holiday Chicken (For Your Pet)   *Michelle Gardner*

The following recipe is from the "CALIFORNIA AMERICAN ESKIMO ASSOC," Newsletter Vol. 7, October 1986 Issue. Put those chicken gizzards to good use and make a pet very happy.

1 1/2 lb. chicken gizzards
    (or turkey giblets)
1 T. vegetable oil
1 c. cooked vegetable (any kind)

1/2 c. rice
1 egg, soft cooked
pinch of garlic salt

Cook gizzards in water until tender. Reserve broth and cook rice in broth. Finely chop gizzards and mix ingredients thoroughly. Use this mixture to season normal diet. Store remaining recipe in the refrigerator.

Golden Pilaf Rice Mix   *Cindy Young*

1 c. uncooked "converted" rice
1/4 c. dried apricots, chopped
1 T. dried minced onion
1 T. chicken bouillon granules

1/3 c. golden raisins
1 t. sugar
1/2 t. white pepper

Combine all ingredients and store in a ziploc bag. To prepare: Combine rice mix with 2 cups water and 2 tablespoons margarine. Bring to a boil; stir. Reduce heat to simmer; cover and cook for 25 minutes, or until rice is tender and liquid is absorbed. Fluff with a fork. Serves 6.

Apple Almond Rice Mix   *Cindy Young*

1 c. uncooked "converted" rice
1/3 c. slivered toasted almonds
1 T. chicken bouillon granules

1/3 c. dried apples, chopped
1 T. parsley flakes

Combine all ingredients and store in a ziploc bag. To prepare: Combine rice mix with 1 cup water, 1 cup apple juice and 1 tablespoon margarine. Reduce heat to simmer; cover and cook for 25 minutes, or until rice is tender and liquid is absorbed. Fluff with a fork. Serves 6.

Dog Treats
Wendy Kronmuller

2 1/2 c. whole wheat flour
2 t. brown sugar
6 T. meat drippings (I use bacon)
1 t. garlic powder
1/2 t. onion powder

1/2 c. powdered dry milk
1 t. beef bouillon
1/2 t. salt
1 egg, beaten
1/2 c. ice water

Preheat oven to 350 degrees. Mix together all ingredients except the meat drippings, egg and water. Cut in the drippings until mixture resembles corn meal. Mix in the egg. Add just enough water to make the mixture form a ball. Pat dough, then roll and cut into shapes, using a dog bone cutter. Bake on a greased cookie sheet for 25 to 30 minutes. Cool and serve.

Sugared Nuts
Brenda Radzinski

4 c. walnuts or pecans
2 egg whites
1 c. sugar

1 1/2 t. cinnamon
1 stick butter

Spread nuts on a cookie sheet and heat at 325 degrees for 10 minutes. Beat egg whites until stiff peaks form. Fold in sugar and cinnamon. After removing nuts from oven, fold into egg white mixture. Put butter on the cookie sheet and allow to melt in oven. Spread coated nuts onto the cookie sheet with the melted butter and stir, making sure they are coated well. Bake for 30 minutes, stirring every 10 minutes. Do not let them get too brown. Cool thoroughly. Store in a sealed container. They make a wonderful gift when placed in a decorated container.

Cran-Apple Jelly

Kathy Bolyea

1 1/2 c. cranapple drink
1/2 c. apple juice
1/8 t. cloves, ground

3 1/2 c. sugar
1/8 t. cinnamon
3 oz. pkg. liquid pectin

Combine sugar, cranapple drink, apple juice, cinnamon and cloves. Bring to a full rolling boil, stirring to dissolve sugar. Boil 1 minute. Remove from heat. Stir in pectin. Ladle into 4, 8-oz. jars. Cool slightly, cover. Let stand several hours at room temperature or until set. Store in refrigerator 3 weeks or freeze up to 3 months.

Spiced Pecans

Kathy Bolyea

1/4 c. margarine
1 1/2 c. sugar
1 T. cinnamon

4 c. pecans
1 T. cloves, ground
1 T. nutmeg, ground

Melt margarine and add pecans. Cook and stir 20 minutes. Drain on paper towels. Mix remaining ingredients in plastic container. Add warm pecans and shake to coat. Spread on a cookie sheet to cool completely. Store in airtight container.

Pumpkin Butter

Kathy Bolyea

16 oz. can pumpkin
1 t. cinnamon
2 1/4 c. sugar

3 T. powdered pectin
1/2 t. allspice

In a 2-qt. microwave bowl, combine pumpkin, pectin, cinnamon and allspice. Mix well. Microwave on HIGH for 6 minutes or until very hot, mixing every 2 minutes. Add sugar, mix well. Microwave on HIGH for 5 to 10 minutes or until full rolling boil, stirring once during cooking. Continue to boil for 1 minute. Spoon into 3 hot 8-oz. jars. Screw lids tight. Store in refrigerator up to 3 weeks or freeze up to 3 months.

The Christmas Groaning Board

Crunchy Caramel Snack Mix
Kathy Bolyea

3 c. chocolate corn puffed cereal
3 c. bite-size oat square cereal
1/2 c. margarine
1/4 c. light corn syrup
1/4 t. cream of tartar

1 c. unsalted peanuts
2 c. small, twisted pretzels
1 c. packed brown sugar
1/4 t. baking soda
1/2 t. vanilla

In a 13" x 9" pan, combine cereals, peanuts and pretzels; set aside. Combine sugar, margarine, and corn syrup. Cook and stir over medium heat until margarine melts and mixture comes to a boil. Cook without stirring for 4 minutes. Remove from heat, stir in baking soda, and cream of tartar. Stir in vanilla. Pour over cereal mixture. Bake at 300 degrees for 30 minutes, stirring after 15 minutes. Transfer to large shallow pan. Cool. Store in airtight container. Makes 10 cups.

Honey Glazed Snack Mix
Kathy Bolyea

4 c. oat square cereal
1 c. pecans
1/4 c. honey

1 1/2 c. twisted pretzels
1/3 c. margarine

In a bowl, combine cereal, pretzels and pecans. Over low heat, melt margarine with honey until margarine melts. Pour over mix; toss to coat. Spread on cookie sheet. Bake at 350 degrees for 15 minutes. Cool and spread on waxed paper.

Christmas Jam
Judy Norris

1 c. fresh cranberries
10 oz. pkg. frozen strawberries
    (thawed)

2 c. sugar

Put cranberries into a blender, cover and chop by turning on and off, on and off, etc. Empty into saucepan, add strawberries and bring to a boil. Add sugar and boil until thickened. (It doesn't thicken alot.) Pour into jelly glasses. Put canning lids on and process according to canning directions. With processing, jam may also be placed in refrigerator for 2 to 4 weeks.

Cinnamon Pecans

Linda Floyd

1 egg white
1 lb. pecans
1 t. salt

1 t. water
1 c. sugar
1 t. cinnamon

Combine egg white and water. Beat until stiff. Add pecans, coating them with the egg mixture. Add sugar, salt and cinnamon, coating well. Place on a cookie sheet and bake at 300 degrees for 25 minutes. Stir after 15 minutes and move cookie sheet to top rack.

Christmas Surprise Candy

Debbie Clement

We make big batches of this candy for our trash collector, our mail person and our newspaper carrier. We like to share the joy of the season and show our appreciation for the people who serve our needs all year long.

1 lb. white almond bark
2 c. spanish peanuts or other nuts

1 c. peanut butter
12 oz. chocolate chips

Melt bark. Add chips and peanut butter, and melt together. Add nuts. Spread thinly on a large sheet of waxed paper. Cool, then refrigerate. Break into bite-sized pieces.

Almond Brittle

Gale Wightman

1 c. sugar
1/4 t. salt
10 oz. pkg. slivered,
    blanched almonds

1/2 c. light corn syrup
2 T. butter
1 t. baking soda

Lightly butter a large cookie sheet. In a heavy 2-qt. saucepan, over medium heat, heat sugar, corn syrup, salt and 1/4 cup of water, to boiling. Stirring constantly until sugar dissolves. Stir in almonds. Continue cooking, stirring frequently, until it reaches hard crack stage (when small amount of mixture dropped in cold water turns brittle). Generally about 20 minutes. As it darkens, stir constantly. Remove pan from heat and stir in butter and baking soda. Immediately pour onto cookie sheet and with 2 forks, pull mixture into a rectangle.

Creamy Fudge

Gale Wightman

5 c. sugar
1 large can evaporated milk
12 oz. chocolate chips
1 large jar marshmallow fluff

1/2 lb. butter
2 t. vanilla
2 c. nuts

Put chips, fluff, vanilla and nuts in a mixing bowl. Heat sugar, butter and milk in a large saucepan. When mixture begins to boil, watch for 15 minutes, stirring often. Check mixture by dropping on ice to make a quick congeal. It may go 20 minutes. Put mixture into mixing bowl containing chips and mix on high speed until creamy. Pour into buttered pan. Will set about 3 to 4 hours.

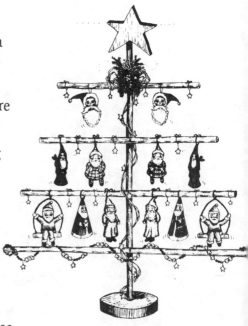

Almond Butter Crunch Wheels
Deborah Evans

1/2 c. butter
1 c. blanched, slivered almonds

1/2 c. sugar
1 T. light corn syrup

Line bottom and sides of an 8" or 9" cake pan with foil, not plastic wrap or waxed paper. Butter foil heavily and set aside. Combine almonds, butter, sugar and corn syrup in a 10" skillet. Bring to a boil over medium heat, stirring constantly, until mixture turns golden brown, about 5 to 6 minutes. Working quickly, spread candy in prepared pan. Cool about 15 minutes, or until firm. Remove from pan and peel off foil. Cool completely. Candy may be broken into pieces or wrapped up as a disk for a yummy holiday gift.

Candied Nuts
Jerrene Rogers

1 c. sugar
1 T. corn syrup

1/4 c. water
3 c. nutmeats

In a small saucepan, combine sugar, water and corn syrup, until sugar is dissolved. Bring to a boil and cook for 1 minute (until a small amount dropped in cold water forms a soft ball). Pour syrup over nutmeats; stir quickly and turn onto a greased cookie sheet. Separate nuts with two forks and let dry. Food coloring can also be added to mixture.

Crazy Crunch
Netta Groat

2 qt. popping corn
2/3 c. almonds
1 c. oleo
1 t. vanilla

1 1/3 c. pecans
1 1/3 c. sugar
1 c. light corn syrup

Mix popped corn and nuts on a cookie sheet. Combine sugar, oleo and corn syrup in saucepan, boil, stirring constantly. Cook 10 to 15 minutes until a light caramel color. Remove and stir in vanilla. Pour over the popped corn and nuts, mix to coat well. Spread out to dry. Break apart and store in a tightly covered container.

The Christmas Groaning Board

Pfeffernusse (Peppernuts)

Laurel Greif

1 c. sugar
1 c. butter
1 t. cinnamon
3/4 t. baking soda (dissolved
    in 1 t. warm water)

1 c. white syrup
4 c. flour
1/4 t. allspice
1/2 t. anise oil

Combine sugar, butter and syrup in a pan, bring to a boil. Cool to luke-warm. Add all the other ingredients and make into a dough. Work dough and roll into long rolls about 3/4" in diameter. Chill rolls or you can freeze. (I find they slice better if frozen.) Slice and bake at 350 to 375 degrees for 8 to 10 minutes or until golden brown. Watch closely as they brown quickly in the last few minutes.

Hard Tack (Christmas Candy)

Dena Cardi

4 c. sugar
1 c. light corn syrup
1 t. flavored (any flavor) oil
    used for candy making

2 c. water
powdered sugar, sifted
food coloring

Cook sugar, water and corn syrup until it reaches 280 degrees on a candy thermometer or until crack stage. Remove from heat and add flavoring and oil. Pour onto greased cookie sheet and allow to cool. When it is cool enough to handle, cut into 1" squares and toss into a deep bowl containing the powdered sugar. Toss the pieces well to coat, then remove them and place into an airtight container. Makes 2 lbs.

Everyone loves cookies at Christmas! Fill a basket, bowl or tin with your grandma's best Christmas cookies and tuck in the recipe for a special surprise.

Nut Crunch Candy   *Dena Cardi*

1 T. light corn syrup   1/2 c. sugar
1 1/2 c. slivered almonds, or   1/2 c. butter
   cashew halves

Mix all the ingredients in a frying pan over medium heat. Stir well and
cook until it turns a butterscotch color (like peanut brittle). Pour onto a
lightly greased cookie sheet and flatten with a wooden spoon. Break into
pieces and store in an airtight container.

Apple Butter   *Dena Cardi*

2 doz. medium apples   3 c. sugar
   (skinned, cored and quartered)   1/2 t. ground cloves
2 qt. apple cider   2 t. ground cinnamon
   (natural, no sugar added)

Cook apples in the cider until tender. Pour into a foley food mill, or use
a food processor, and grind into pulp. Cook pulp until thick enough to
round in a spoon, stirring frequently. Add spices and sugar. Cook over
medium-low heat for another hour, until thick. Pour into 1/2-pt. canning
jars that have been processed in a hot water bath. Fill the jars up to about
1/2" from top. Use processed lids to top jars, tighten slightly, then process
jars in hot water canning bath for 10 minutes. Remove from water and
allow to cool, then tighten lids. Check tops to see that they have "popped"
down. Apple Butter will keep for 6 months or more on the shelf. Makes
8 jars.

The Christmas Groaning Board

Homemade Applebutter
Karen Perry

12 c. applesauce
1/4 c. vinegar
10 oz. bag red cinnamon drops

9 c. sugar
1/4 c. lemon juice

Place ingredients in a pan and boil until thick. Reduce heat to low and simmer for 2 to 3 hours. Stir

Homemade Vanilla Extract
Cheryl Livesay

A perfect gift for friends that like to bake.

1 c. inexpensive brandy
2 vanilla beans, cut into 2" pieces

Combine the brandy and vanilla beans in a jar with a tight-fitting lid. Cover and let stand for 3 months, shaking weekly. Makes 1 cup.

Once you get your first batch of vanilla mellowed, you can continue to use the beans. Once you've used a tablespoon or so, just pour more brandy into the jar to keep the level up. After using about 3/4 cup of the extract, throw in a new bean. Besides producing a superior tasting vanilla extract, making your own will cost less than buying the commercial version.

Caramel Corn
Susan Kirschenheiter

1 c. margarine
1 t. salt
1/2 c. light corn syrup
1 t. baking soda

2 c. brown sugar
6 qt. popped corn
1/4 t. cream of tartar
vanilla

Mix butter, white syrup and brown sugar; bring to a boil. Let boil for 6 minutes, keep stirring. Take off heat and add cream of tartar, salt, baking soda and vanilla. Stir until foamy and pour this on popped corn. Spread this on a cookie sheet, after mixing well. Bake at 200 degrees for 1 hour. (Use a big kettle when cooking, because this foams up big.)

Sugared Pecans In Double Batches
Michele Roudebush

Every Christmas my mom made Sugared Pecans in double batches because they are so good that one batch is eaten as fast as they come from the oven.

2 egg whites
pinch of salt
1/2 c. butter or margarine

1 c. sugar
3 1/2 c. whole pecans
sprinkle of cinnamon

Place butter or margarine in a 15" x 10" x 1" baking pan. Bake at 325 degrees until melted, about 5-7 minutes. Meanwhile in a mixing bowl, beat egg whites until stiff. Add the sugar and salt; beat. Fold in the pecans. Pour over butter and toss to coat. Bake at 300 degrees for 30 minutes, stirring every 10 minutes. Remove from oven and sprinkle with cinnamon.

Nutmeg Sauce
Michele Roudebush

2 c. sugar
2 T. cornstarch or 3 T. flour
   (both heaping)
2 1/2 to 3 c. water

2 T. butter
1/2 t. cinnamon
1/4 t. nutmeg
dash of salt

Boil all ingredients until thick. Serve warm.

The Christmas Groaning Board

Edna's Hard Sauce
Lee Charrier

1 lb. confectioners sugar less 3T.
2 T. vegetable shortening
1/4 c. brandy

3/4 stick of butter
2 t. vanilla

Mix together the sugar, butter and shortening, adding the vanilla half-way through. Moisten with brandy. Beat with fork, cover and refrigerate. Remove from refrigerator 1 hour before serving. When ready to serve, sprinkle with brandy. Stir and beat with fork into a serving dish. Dust with nutmeg. Super with good plum pudding, hot and flambed.

Toffee
Mary Anne Perks

1 c. butter
1 c. walnuts, finely chopped

1 c. sugar
6 oz. chocolate chips

Butter well a 9" square pan. Combine butter and sugar in a heavy saucepan, cook over moderate heat, stirring constantly, until mixture reaches 310 degrees on a candy thermometer. Candy should be caramel colored and a small drop of mixture should form a hard ball when dropped into cold water. Remove from heat when testing. Quickly pour candy into the pan and spread evenly. Cool until hardened. Melt 1/2 of the chocolate chips over hot water and spread on top of candy. Sprinkle with nuts. When chocolate is hardened, turn candy onto waxed paper. Cover with remaining chocolate and nuts. Break cooled candy into pieces. Store in a tightly covered tin. Makes 1 lb.

Mother's Peanut Brittle
Elizabeth Heyman

This is my mother's (Mary Schmeltzer) recipe. She made upwards of 200 lbs. each Christmas and it was enjoyed by many people. She was the mother of 12 children, and has been deceased for 3 years.

2 c. white sugar
1/2 c. water
1 T. oleo (heaping)

1 c. light corn syrup
2 t. baking soda
2 c. raw peanuts

Cook sugar, corn syrup and water over hot flame until temperature reaches 230 degrees on the candy thermometer. Add peanuts and continue cooking and stirring frequently until thermometer reaches 298 to 300 degrees. Remove from fire AT ONCE, add baking soda and oleo. Stir just enough to melt oleo and dissolve soda. At once, pour on a large, well greased tray (I use a lasagne pan). Do not spread out. Let it go where it will. Cool outside, then break in pieces. Use heavy saucepan and wooden spoon. Temperature outside should be freezing or colder and clear.

Chocolate Covered Apricots
Sheryl Adams

1/2 c. brandy
1/2 c. sugar
semi-sweet or bittersweet chocolate

1/2 c. vodka
dried apricots

In a quart jar, pour the brandy, vodka and sugar. Stir until dissolved. Pack in dried apricots. Let soak for four to six weeks, turning every week. Dry off on paper towels, then dip in chocolate. Chill on cookie sheet until chocolate hardens.

The Christmas Groaning Board

Grace's Bourbon Balls
Lee Charrier

1 1/4 c. finely chopped or
    ground pecans
2 1/2 c. crushed vanilla wafers
    (12 oz. box makes 3 c. measure)

2 T. unsweetened cocoa
2 T. dark corn syrup
1/3 c. bourbon

Mix ingredients and pinch together with hands. With powdered sugar on hands, roll into 1" balls.

1/4 c. confectioners sugar
1/2 c. sugar

2 T. cocoa

Mix together and place in a soup dish or a pie tin. Roll balls in mixture. Store in tins lined with waxed paper. Sprinkle remaining sugar mix over all. Do not serve for at least 2 weeks. Great if frozen a month ahead.

Herb Butter
Judy Carter

1/2 lb. butter
2 t. chives, snipped finely
1/4 t. sage

4 T. parsley
2 t. lemon juice

Cream butter. Add chives, sage, parsley and lemon juice.

A loaf of homemade bread and a crock of herb butter—always a welcomed gift!

Sweet Hot Mustard
Betty Richmond

1/4 lb. container dry mustard
3 c. flour
3 eggs, beaten
2 1/4 c. vinegar

1 1/2 c. sugar
1 1/4 t. salt
1 1/2 T. margarine, melted

Mix together mustard, sugar, flour and salt. Gradually add vinegar. Add eggs and margarine last, mixing well. Let stand uncovered overnight. Makes about 4, 1/2-pt. jelly glasses.

Chocolate-Flavored Powdered Drink Mix
Diane Dollak

A bag of drink mix (with miniature marshmallows added for festivity of course) tied with a ribbon, and presented with a mug and cookies makes a wonderful gift.

5 1/3 c. dry milk powder
1 jar powdered drink mix (chocolate or malt flavored)

Mix together and store in a cannister. When ready to serve, measure 4 to 5 heaping teaspoonsful into a mug, add boiling water (and marshmallows, if you like) and serve.

Pancake and Waffle Mix
Susan Kirschenheiter

Basic Mix:
6 c. flour
6 T. baking powder
6 T. sugar

2 c. powdered milk
1 T. salt

To Make Batter:
1 1/2 c. basic mix
1 c. water

1 egg, beaten
2 T. vegetable oil

Beat ingredients with a fork. Fry in a tiny bit of oil in a skillet. For nutrition add 2 tablespoons raw wheat germ to batter.

Great to give packed in an airtight container along with the recipe and a pitcher of delicious maple syrup!

197

APPETIZERS
Almond Pinecones, 105
Angels on Horseback, 97
Bean Dip, 96
Cheese Spread, 102
Cheese-Do-Floppies, 93
Crab Dip, 92
Crabbies, 95
Crunchy Caramel Snack Mix, 186
Debbie's Long-Distance Michigan Corn
    Chip Dip, 95
Garlic Spread, 98
Ham and Swiss Rolls, 94
Herbed Popcorn, 95
Holiday Spread, 101
Honey Glazed Snack Mix, 186
Mexican Ole!, 98
Mushroom Appetizer Squares, 94
Shrimp & Crab Cheese Dip, 104
Spicy Cheese Ball, 96
Tasty Chip Dip, 92

BEEF
Fool Proof Prime Rib, 122
Glazed Corned Beef, 120
Meatballs with Sweet and Sour Sauce,
    103

BEVERAGES
Chocolate Coffee, 101
Chocolate-Flavored Powdered Drink
    Mix, 197
Christmas Eve Sneaky Petes, 105
Festive Eggnog Punch, 102
Grapefruit Slush, 97
Holiday Mulled Punch, 100
Hot Buttered Rum, 101
Hot Chocolate Mix, 105
Hot Cranberry Punch, 99
Hot Pilgrim, 100
Hot Spiced Wine Punch, 102
Mocha Nog, 104
Mulled Tea Bags, 92
Patrick's Holiday Egg Nog, 99
Punch, 96
Russian Tea, 103
Sonia's Holiday Sangria 98

Spiced Percolator Punch, 99
Spiced Tea, 93
Swedish Cream, 97
Wassail, 106

BREADS
Annie's Famous Pumpkin Bread, 113
Apple Bread, 115
Beaumond Bread, 110
Cherry Blossom Muffins, 112
Chocolate Chip Zucchini Bread, 109
Chocolate-Banana Bread, 159
Christmas Morning Cinnamon Rolls,
    114
Cinnamon Nut Loaf, 111
Cinnamon Sticks "1886", 147
Date Loaf, 109
Granma Lesieur's Mouth Watering
    "Banana Nut Bread", 113
Lemon Fruitcake or Bread, 115
Orange Bran Loaf, 112
Pancake and Waffle Mix, 197
Poppyseed Bread, 116
Pumpkin Bread, 110
Rotterdam Banket, 178
Southern Biscuit Muffins, 111
Wonderful Pecan Rolls, 116

CAKES
Cheesecake Cupcakes, 158
Chocolate Sheet Cake, 146
Christmas Fruitcake, 149
Dump Cake, 155
Grandma Dixon's Applespice Cake, 157
Holiday Fruitcake, 141
Kentucky Whiskey Cake, 145
Mexican Fruitcake, 155
New Year's Cakes, 176
Old-Fashioned Shortcake, 175
Old-Fashioned Tea Cakes, 145
Orange Pudding Cake, 160
Orange Slice Cake, 163
Pumpkin Cake Roll, 139
Pumpkin Fruitcake, 157
Scripture Cake, 140
Whoopie Pies, 151

Yuletide Menus ☆ Open House ☆ Stocking Stuffers ☆ Memories ☆ Christmas Crafts ☆ Celebrations & Events ☆ My Wish List ☆ Memories ☆ Recipes ☆ Decorating Ideas ☆ Holiday Hints ☆ Gift Lists ☆ Traditions ☆ Christmas Cards ☆

☆ Yuletide Menus ☆ Open House ☆ Stocking Stuffers ☆ Memories ☆ Christmas Crafts ☆ Celebrations & Events ☆ My Wish List ☆ Recipes ☆ Memories ☆ Recipes ☆ Decorating ideas ☆ Holiday Hints ☆ Gift Lists ☆ Traditions ☆ Christmas Cards ☆

Yuletide Menus ☆ Open House ☆ Stocking Stuffers ☆ Memories ☆ Christmas Crafts ☆ Celebrations & Events ☆ My Wish List ☆ Memories ☆ Recipes ☆ Memories ☆ Decorating ideas ☆ Holiday Hints ☆ Gift Lists ☆ Traditions ☆ Christmas Cards ☆

☆ Yuletide Menus ☆ Open House ☆ Stocking Stuffers ☆ Memories ☆ Christmas Crafts ☆ Celebrations & Events ☆ My Wish List ☆ Memories ☆ Recipes ☆ Decora-ting ideas ☆ Holiday Hints ☆ Gift Lists☆ Traditions ☆ Christmas Cards☆

☆ Yuletide Menus ☆   Open House ☆ Stocking Stuffers ☆ Memories ☆ Christmas Crafts ☆ Celebrations & Events ☆ My Wish List ☆ Memories ☆ Recipes ☆ Decorating ideas ☆ Holiday Hints ☆ Gift Lists ☆ Traditions ☆ Christmas Cards ☆

☆ Yuletide Menus ☆ Open House ☆ Stocking Stuffers ☆ Memories ☆ Christmas Crafts ☆ Celebrations & Events ☆ My Wish List ☆ Memories ☆ Recipes ☆ Decorating ideas ☆ Holiday Hints ☆ Gift Lists ☆ Traditions ☆ Christmas Cards ☆

We've cooked up a whole collection of Gooseberry Patch™ books!

Have a taste for more? Call us toll-free at
1-800-854-6673

We'll send you our latest catalog filled with snowmen, Santas, ornaments, candles, cookie cutters, gourmet goodies, salt-glazed pottery collectibles and MORE...including our best-selling cookbooks!

Phone us:
1·800·854·6673

Fax us:
1·740·363·7225

Visit our website:
www.gooseberrypatch.com

Send us your favorite recipe!

and the memory that makes it special for you! * We're putting together a brand new **Gooseberry Patch** cookbook, and you're invited to participate. If we select your recipe, your name will appear right along with it...and you'll receive a FREE copy of the book! Mail to:

Vickie & Jo Ann
Gooseberry Patch, Dept. BOOK
P.O. Box 190
Delaware, Ohio 43015

*Please help us by including the number of servings and all other necessary information!

Yuletide Menus ☆ Open House ☆ Stocking Stuffers ☆ Memories ☆ Christmas Crafts ☆ Celebrations & Events ☆ My Wish List ☆ Memories ☆ Recipes ☆ Decorating ideas ☆ Holiday Hints ☆ Gift Lists ☆ Traditions ☆ Christmas Cards ☆